	DATE DUE		

Travel and Entertainment Best Practices

TRAVEL AND ENTERTAINMENT BEST PRACTICES

MARY S. SCHAEFFER

JOHN WILEY & SONS, INC.

This book is printed on acid-free paper.♾

Copyright © 2007 by Mary S. Schaeffer All rights reserved.

Published by John Wiley & Sons, Inc., Hoboken, New Jersey.
Published simultaneously in Canada.

For general information on our other products and services please contact our Customer Care Department within the U.S. at 877-762-2974, outside the U.S. at 317-572-3993, or fax 317-572-4002.

Wiley also publishes its books in a variety of electronic formats. Some content that appears in print, however, may not be available in electronic format.

For more information about Wiley products, visit our Web site at http://www.wiley.com.

Library of Congress Cataloging-in-Publication Data:

Schaeffer, Mary S.
   Travel and entertainment best practices / Mary S. Schaeffer.
        p. cm.
   Includes index.
   ISBN-13: 978-0-470-044827 (cloth)
   ISBN-10: 0-470-04482-9 (cloth)
   1. Business travel—Management. 2. Travel costs. I. Title.
   G156.5.B86S33 2007
   658.15′5—dc22

                                   2006025755

Printed in the United States of America.

10 9 8 7 6 5 4 3 2 1

For my husband, Hal Schaeffer, a man who always gets his T&E reports done on time!

CONTENTS

PREFACE

When I told my family that I had signed a contract to write a book about travel and entertainment (T&E), they let out a collective sigh of relief. "Finally—a book that's not about that boring business stuff you usually write about," was what they said. As you can see, tact is not their strong suit.

I'm afraid they were both right and wrong. While I think this stuff is interesting, I don't think it is quite what they had in mind. This is a book about both internal controls and cost control; not a book about exotic travel as my family had envisioned.

It is also a book about change; and for once, most of that change is good. If you have not reviewed the way your organization handles its T&E function, including the booking, approval, reporting, and reimbursement processes, you may be in for a big surprise. There have been some phenomenal developments, some of which just might pleasantly surprise you. The competition for the business traveler remains cutthroat and for once, the traveler and his or her organization are the winners.

This is not to say that the process is without its headaches. Some of the old chestnuts remain. Getting people to fill out expense reports after a trip continues to be a challenge, many managers continue to approve any report put in front of them without even glancing at the contents and yes, crooked employees still look for ways to cheat their employers via their T&E expenses.

The book begins with an overview of the factors that have played a role in the evolution of the T&E function. There are a number and their influence has been far reaching. It then goes on to briefly discuss how the function is handled and a number of the problems that pervade the function and will affect various aspects as discussed further in the book.

We then move on to take a look at the booking function. While you may at first think this is a humdrum topic not worthy of inclusion, you will be astounded when you see the changes and breakthroughs that are occurring in this area.

The book also addresses what might be the most poorly attended function and the one that often causes many of the non-compliance issues and allows fraud. That is the approval process, or more to the point, the incorrect application of the approval functionality.

The review and reimbursement process is typically handled with more attention than the approval process and this can cause headaches for the professionals responsible for that function. They often find themselves between a rock and a hard place when managers approve travel items in direct conflict with the written corporate T&E policy. Suggestions on how to address this issue are offered.

It will come as no surprise to those reading this to learn that the IRS has something to say about how T&E expenses and reimbursements are handled. This is an important issue to understand. The appropriate IRS requirements need to be incorporated into the organization's policy if the company doesn't want to lose its plan's status as an accountable plan. Incorporating it into the plan is just the first step. The organization needs to make sure that these requirements are met by its employees, so compliance in the areas that affect a plan's status is very important. There can be income tax implications.

We also look at how companies pay for their travel, discussing in depth the pros and cons of the various approaches. A look at corporate T&E cards and the impact of rebates on corporate purchasing cards and how that is affecting T&E card functionality is included.

Getting receipts and proper documentation is not only a matter of company policy, it is a matter of law if an organization is to take deductions on its income tax returns, which virtually all do. Thus, there is a discussion of what needs to be done when it comes to obtaining, handling, and storing receipts for items your travelers claim on their expense reports.

The organization's T&E policy and procedure manual is a vital part of a program that demonstrates strong internal controls. It is also the organization's defense against rogue spending by an employee. And, after the passage of the Sarbanes-Oxley Act (SOX), not having a good policy is likely to get the organization dinged in its SOX audit. The issues of updating the policy, sharing the information with all affected employees, and the uniform administration of that policy are also investigated. Sample wording for some of the sections of a policy are offered to help readers create their own policy manual.

We then move on to an investigation of the day-to-day problems that affect the processing of T&E reports, offering solutions to the headaches that vex the staff responsible for the processing of this information. While some of the problems may seem trivial at first glance, they are anything but for the groups that have to deal with them first hand.

Unfortunately, fraud is a fact of life that affects most organizations when it comes to T&E expense reporting and requests for reimbursement. In many cases it is petty and the dollars involved are not large. Regrettably, when employees get away with the fraud once, they are often emboldened and steal more the second time and each additional trip, until they are caught. Thus, when the final tally is complete, the employees have often stolen thousands of dollars from the organization. We've got a number of real-life stories, as well as a look at some common ways employees try to steal and then some solutions.

There is also a discussion of the corporate policy as it affects the treatment of such thefts. They range from immediate dismissal for even the smallest infraction deemed to be theft, to some policies that are quite lenient in allowing the employee to make restitution over a period of time.

Automation is making a big impact on T&E reporting and it is helping with a number of other issues discussed in the book. We'll take a look at what's going on and how it is impacting the T&E reporting, review, and reimbursement functions.

The book also contains a chapter that addresses a few of the issues that both your international travelers and the staff who process their returns will face. It also contains a thorough discussion of one of the few areas where the professionals handle T&E processing.

Finally, for those large organizations with significant travel spend, we'll offer some advice for negotiating contracts for employee travel. If there is a large dollar spend, it is possible to negotiate contracts that will save the organization quite a bit.

We'll end the book with a chapter that spells out today's best practices when it comes to T&E expense reporting, approval, review, and reimbursement. I say *today's* best practices because the space is changing so rapidly that what is best practice today will change within a few short years.

I wish you the best of luck with your T&E processes.

Mary Schaeffer
January 2007

ACKNOWLEDGMENTS

Clearly I wouldn't have all the great information in this book if numerous Accounts Payable professionals hadn't been willing to share with me their experiences, both good and bad. I am grateful to them not only for the information they provided but also for the entertainment. Many of the stories are amusing as well as instructive. They are shared not only because they are funny but because they demonstrate just where the loopholes are in a weak travel and entertainment process and point out changes that need to be made.

This book would not have been possible without the support of the staff of John Wiley & Sons and the very fine editor I have been lucky enough to work with, Sheck Cho. I thank them all for their support on this and other projects.

1

TRAVEL AND ENTERTAINMENT EXPENSE POLICY AND REIMBURSEMENT PROCESS: NOT WHAT IT WAS A FEW SHORT YEARS AGO

INTRODUCTION

Travel and entertainment (T&E) expenses are the second largest controllable expense for most organizations. Hence, the process should get a lot of attention. Yet, until very recently (think Sarbanes-Oxley) it was one of the last bastions of unfettered bad employee behavior with even very respectable companies allowing practices that you would have thought ended decades ago.

The T&E reimbursement process is a cost function, not adding anything to the bottom line. It is one of those petty annoying functions that brings little praise or glory when things run smoothly but can force the spotlight on a group when things go wrong—especially if the story ends up in the newspapers, as has happened several times in recent years.

Thus, organizations everywhere are starting to change their poor T&E practices. There are a number of reasons for this. Before we start our investigation into the nitty-gritty of the T&E expense function, let's take a look at some of the trends that are causing change in this necessary, but sometimes irksome, corporate function.

TRENDS AFFECTING T&E EXPENSE REPORTING

Twenty years ago, cash advances and paper expense reports were the norm. There was no other way to travel. This made the travel and entertainment reimbursement process cumbersome and subject to human error. Calculation errors were frequent and compiling data for any sort of analysis was almost impossible. The specter of clerks surrounded by mountains of paper as they review reports and check math has all but disappeared. Here are some of the reasons:

- T&E cards
- No more cash advances
- Internet
- Sarbanes-Oxley Act
- Automation
- Cost control
- Policy compliance
- Visibility factor
- Fraud

- Changing cultures
- Exhaustion of corporate tolerance

T&E Cards

A large number of companies give their traveling employees credit cards to use for company business. These cards can be used for meals, hotels, transportation, and a variety of other items, whether the employee is away from home or in town. The cards remove the onus of the employee using his or her own credit cards, although many companies still do not provide these cards.

No More Cash Advances

The aforementioned T&E cards along with a growing number of places that take the cards have made cash advances far less necessary than in the past. According to a recent survey by *Accounts Payable Now & Tomorrow*, less than half the companies responding offer their employees cash advances. Even in those that do, the dollar amounts are often restricted and the circumstances under which they are given further limit the use of cash advances. Companies have found another reason to eliminate advances. Employees who have forked out their own funds are much more likely to complete their T&E expense reports on a timely basis than are those who have to return funds to the company.

Internet

Without a doubt, the Internet has affected the way employees book travel. Not only has it made it simpler to have employees book their own flights, it has given them the tool needed to shop for less expensive options as well as check on plans made by their travel agents. This can be both a blessing and a curse. While it helps keep travel agents honest, it also has led to employees who search for travel savings to the detriment of overall travel programs. The Internet has also introduced automation into a function that was largely paper based. Unfortunately, it helps deceitful employees intent on defrauding their employers of a few bucks. This issue will be discussed in detail in Chapter 11.

Sarbanes-Oxley Act

The last five to ten years have not been kind to the corporate world. The shameful behavior of a few has cast a spotlight onto practices of the entire business population, forcing, in some cases, much needed change. One of those areas has been T&E. In fact, in the same *Accounts Payable Now & Tomorrow* study mentioned earlier, 57% of those responding indicated they had changed their T&E policies because of the passage of the Sarbanes-Oxley Act. Particularly interesting about this statistic is that only 30% of those responding to the survey were public companies. Sarbanes-Oxley has served as a wakeup call to organizations everywhere that they need to clean up their act when it comes to T&E—and apparently many heeded the call. In fact, when asked about the frequency of policy updates, a number of respondents said things like, "this is the first time we've ever done one," "working on it now," and "currently updating."

Automation

Very few companies still rely on a paper form for T&E reporting. At a minimum, most use an Excel-based form. In fact, in the *Accounts Payable Now & Tomorrow* survey, almost half of those responding indicated they used an Excel-based form. Only 15% still use that paper form. This means that the time spent checking the calculations is eliminated from the review process—assuming of course that the formulas for the calculations are locked. Otherwise, unscrupulous employees can adjust their returns. It means that organizations either can have fewer employees reviewing T&E reports and processing them or they can have the same number but these employees can spend their time looking for policy compliance or analysing the data. In either event, the staff working on T&E can use their time for more productive tasks.

Cost Control

As companies look for ways to cut costs, it is no surprise that T&E has come under scrutiny. Larger companies have long negotiated favorable rates with preferred carriers, and this continues both for air travel and lodging. Use of per diems is another way that companies reign in spending when it comes to meals. The amounts used for per diems are usually based on government published rates and can lead to a lot of complaints from the employees who are subject to them. But, if cost control is a serious issue, per diems are the way to go.

Policy Compliance

Policy compliance is now a huge issue, both for those looking to keep costs under control, as discussed above, and those looking to ensure tight internal controls. The aforementioned automation has made policy compliance easier to monitor in certain instances. Some of the third-party T&E services have built-in policy compliance checking routines. Many of these simply will not allow employees to enter reimbursement requests outside the policy limits. Companies looking to avoid spectacles when some of their executives' freewheeling expenses are made public are cracking down on those who don't comply with the written policy.

Visibility Factor

Automation, the Internet, and some of the recent corporate debacles have made T&E expenditures more visible. Companies are now able to run reports that show who spent how much on what. They highlight policy non-compliance. These reports, while always part of third-party products, are now more commonplace. Companies now have access to information they need to monitor what's going on as well as to use in negotiating contracts with preferred suppliers.

Fraud

Before you dismiss T&E fraud, let me point out several factors. First, fraud is most frequently committed by long-term, trusted employees. Second, according to the Association of Certified Fraud Examiners' *2004 Report to the Nation*, 22.1% of all fraudulent disbursements were expense reimbursements. The average cost for these cases was $92,000. The cost is so high because T&E fraud generally does not happen once, but is an ongoing event with the crooks getting bolder over time.

Changing Cultures

How all the issues related to T&E are addressed and handled will depend partially on the corporate culture. While a few issues in T&E are black and white, many have some leeway. For example, whether to offer cash advances, whether to have the company or the employee responsible for the credit card bill, and what expenses to cover (e.g., liquor) are just a few of the issues that need written policies so employees know what they can and cannot do. What may seem like a given in one situation will not fly in the next. Benevolent organizations are changing their stripes due to mergers, acquisitions, or harsh business conditions. These and other circumstances will radically change the way an organization treats T&E expenditures of its employees on corporate business. It is imperative that employees are informed of any changes.

Exhaustion of Corporate Tolerance

Given the unsympathetic public reaction to some of the corporate extravagances as well as ruthless cost pressures and the piercing spotlight on internal controls, organizations everywhere are saying, "Enough!" and are ending bad practices. While it is not the business of an organization to monitor employee behavior when it comes to things like hiding income from spouses, most organizations will no longer adjust their reimbursement practices to accommodate these requests from employees.

OTHER ISSUES AFFECTING THE T&E EXPENSE PROCESS

Unfortunately, there is much about the T&E process that is not uniform from one organization to the next. This is true today as much as it was 20 years ago. The main factors influencing this include:

- Human factor
- Personal issues
- Corporate culture

Human Factor

The allure of a quick buck is attractive to a few employees who try and steal from the company via their T&E reports. Since the dollar amounts are usually small, it is often difficult to determine whether the employee simply made an honest mistake or if there was an intent to steal. Thus, fraud detection routines are part of the T&E discussion going forward and are a significant part of this book.

Personal Issues

Employees often use their T&E reimbursements to hide income from their spouses. While it should be beyond the purveyance of the corporate world to make judgments on its employees' behavior, companies are well within their rights to refuse to undertake policies that enable questionable behavior if it means that their operations run less efficiently.

In the past, when reimbursement was done by check hand delivered to the employee, this was an issue between the employee and his or her partner. This is no longer the case. As companies put in more efficient processes, this issue has become a sore point in those organizations that have long tolerated this really poor practice.

Corporate Culture

T&E is one area that has felt the impact of corporate culture on its policies and procedures. Its effects can be seen in how the company addresses some of the following T&E-related issues:

- Cash advances
- How expenses are reimbursed
- Levels of per diems
- Who can fly first class
- Whether a company has a corporate T&E card for its traveling employees or expects them to use their own
- What's reimbursable

- Policy on liquor
- How rogue travelers are treated
- How T&E cheating is treated

OTHER BAD PRACTICES THAT PLAGUE T&E

Possibly more than any other facet of the corporate accounting world, T&E is beleaguered with poor practices. Following is a list of practices that should be avoided. Most will be discussed in detail, along with ways to avoid or eliminate the problem, further along in the book. The bad practices are:

- Not having a written T&E policy
- Not reviewing and updating the T&E policy at least annually
- Not sharing the policy with all affected parties
- Not requiring timely submission of T&E reports
- Tolerating managers who approve reports without reviewing them
- Not requiring receipts for expenses in excess of a policy limit
- Uneven enforcement of the T&E policy
- Reimbursing employees by hand delivering a check
- Not doing spot fraud checks

OUTSIDER'S VIEW

On the face of it, the T&E reimbursement process seems simple enough. An employee travels on company business. She accumulates some expenses and when she returns she fills out an expense reimbursement report, which her manager reviews and approves. It is then usually sent to Accounts Payable so the employee can be reimbursed for her expenses. While it does occasionally work this way, a large percentage of the time it does not.

WORST-CASE SCENARIO

Here's a worst-case scenario that demonstrates what goes wrong. Now, before you start reading, let me say for the record that rarely does everything that is delineated in this example occur on one expense report.

An employee, let's say a salesperson (as they are reputed to be among the worst when it comes to T&E), goes on a business trip to visit clients. While on the trip he takes the clients to dinner and then out for an evening of fun. The fun may be a baseball game or very occasionally a visit to a strip club. Yes, a few rogue salespersons have been known to take clients to such places and then act surprised when the company refuses to reimburse them for the bill. Inevitably, at every Accounts Payable conference I attend—and I go to anywhere from 5 to 12 a year—there is some poor Accounts Payable manager with a story of how he or she had a knock-down drag-out with a salesperson over reimbursement for some questionable entertainment.

Anyway, when the salesperson returns home and eventually compiles his reimbursement request, he does one of two things with the bill from the strip club. He either boldfacedly enters it on the report and requests reimbursement or tries to hide it in a number of creative ways that will be delved into in Chapter 11. Additionally, in our worst-case scenario, he may request reimbursement based on receipts either that he manufactured himself or that came from another event. Sometimes, against company policy, the employee may bring along a family member.

Now, you may be thinking that the boss will refuse to approve the reimbursement, but that is where the next problem occurs.

Most superiors do not review T&E reimbursement requests put in front of them by their employees. They sign whatever the request is. This leads to extremely uneven enforcement of company policy and is unfair. But, it is a reality that most companies are faced with.

So now, our rogue salesperson has a T&E reimbursement request that includes charges at a strip club and this request has been approved when it hits Accounts Payable. Accounts Payable, if it checks reports against the company T&E policy, then has a fight on its hands if it tries to refuse the reimbursement. If it takes the stance that since it is approved it will pay the reimbursement, the company pays for something that it shouldn't.

While this is an extreme case, there are many other less blatant, but equally inappropriate, charges that regularly show up on employees' expense reports. Also, in this example, the employee is basically honest, if not exercising the best judgment. There are those who regularly cheat on their reimbursement requests.

BEST-CASE SCENARIO

The employee goes on a business trip. Within a few days of returning the employee fills out the requisite forms, attaches receipts to document those expenses as required by company policy, and submits the form to his or her boss for approval. This may be done on paper or electronically, if the firm uses an electronic model for T&E.

Within a few days, the manager reviews and approves the report and sends it to Accounts Payable for reimbursement. This reimbursement will take place as mandated by the company policy. This can be as frequently as daily or as infrequently as monthly. Most companies reimburse once a week or once every two weeks. A few organizations do it as part of payroll.

REALITY

The employee takes a trip. One of two scenarios happens, the impact being the same in Accounts Payable or whatever unit is responsible for handling T&E reimbursements. Either the employee fills out the report and gives it to his supervisor relatively quickly after the end of the trip and the manager never gets around to reviewing and approving it, or the employee waits until the credit card bill is due and then the fun begins.

The employee needs the reimbursement funds to pay the credit card bill, so he pesters Accounts Payable for reimbursement. To be reasonable, if the boss has been delinquent in approving the expense report, it is not fair to her employees to make them pay the bills out of their own pocket. However, if the employee just never got around to submitting the expense report, it is an entirely different matter.

Unfortunately, the effect on Accounts Payable is the same. The employee needs a Rush check, and that is a poor policy from a control standpoint and an extremely inefficient use of the Accounts Payable associate's time. If the company had used one of the online electronic T&E models, a lot of these problems would be avoided, especially if it contained one of the escalation features related to the approval process.

And depending on the organization, a good percentage of reports are submitted within a reasonable timeframe, avoiding the problems discussed earlier, although the reports themselves may contain errors.

WHO HANDLES T&E?

Do you ever wonder how your organization stacks up against others? Do you sometimes think that your company is the only one lagging behind when it comes to adopting best practices?

Or do you suspect your Accounts Payable department is ahead of the eight ball? When it comes to T&E, it is often difficult to find data against which to measure your department. Recently, *Accounts Payable Now & Tomorrow* conducted an exhaustive survey to find relevant T&E information. Here we delve into the basics: where T&E is handled.

The handling of T&E is an Accounts Payable function at most companies. When asked where the responsibility for T&E reimbursements lay within their firm, participants responded as follows:

Accounts payable alone	75.7%
Separate T&E department	6.8%
Payroll	2.7%
Accounts payable shared with another group	9.4%
Other	5.4%

At over 85% of those firms surveyed, Accounts Payable had either full or partial responsibility for this function. Thus, throughout this book, when discussing the group responsible for the T&E review and reimbursement function we will refer to Accounts Payable. Know that if there is a separate group that handles it in your organization we are referring to that group.

2

HOW CORPORATE TRAVEL IS BOOKED

INTRODUCTION

Booking corporate travel might be the corporate-travel-related area that is undergoing the most change. As you will see in the ensuing discussion, the number of ways that organizations can arrange for their employees to book their business travel is expanding. For the most part, cost cutting is the impetus for some of these changes.

The size of the corporate travel budget will play a large part in determining what type of booking operation is used for employee travel. The bigger budgets will naturally get more attention and may make use of an entire staff devoted to making arrangements or perhaps a third-party service provider.

There has been an ongoing evolution in this arena and it continues today. At one time, no matter how small an organization, there was still a requirement that a travel professional be used to make travel arrangements. Smaller organizations would give their travelers the contact information for their travel agent. If the organization had slightly more travel, this might have been done through the Human Resources department. Firms where there was a significant amount of travel often had staff devoted exclusively to this task. In any event, rarely did employees make their own plane or hotel reservations.

The Internet changed all that. Employees could check flights and fares. Occasionally they would even discover that their travel agent, who was often compensated on a commission determined by the cost of the airfare, had not given them the least expensive flight.

There is no standard method for booking travel. It varies from organization to organization. If you have a requirement that the travel must be booked through either your travel office or a third-party service provider designated by the company, this should be spelled out in the policy and procedures manual. Otherwise, you will end up with rogue employees who search the Internet for better deals or schedules more to their pleasing and less attractive to your pocketbook.

PRE-TRIP AUTHORIZATIONS

In theory, all business trips should be approved before the expenditure for airlines, hotels, conference attendance, and so forth is contracted for. However, most experts feel this is a waste of time and effort. The reason is simple. The number of employees who would plan and take a trip without their supervisor's approval is extremely limited.

Therefore, although some organizations still do go through the formal process of having all trips authorized beforehand, most have eliminated this step from the travel review process. If your organization is one that still requires the pre-trip approval, make sure to spell out your requirements in the policy.

The policy should not only indicate that a pre-trip approval is required, but also indicate who can approve such trips and how much in advance they should be obtained. If you have a form that you would like used, this should be included in the manual. The advantage of these forms is that there is uniformity in the approval process.

ROLE OF THE TRAVEL AGENT

While travel agents used to be required for all travel, their number is rapidly dwindling. The mid-size companies who relied on them heavily have moved in large part to self-booking over the Internet. This is especially true for domestic travel.

Travel agents do come in handy if the trip is overseas or there is something unusual about the trip, although this advantage may dwindle as the online travel sites continue to become more flexible and expand their options.

CORPORATE TRAVEL OFFICES

Larger organizations have long had corporate travel offices. These offices made travel arrangements for employees who needed to take trips, negotiated with preferred suppliers, and more or less (at least as far as air travel was concerned) assured policy compliance. With a travel office involved, the employee does not have the ability to book a flight that is outside the policy, i.e. first class, when coach is called for. The full-service aspect of a corporate travel office, while comforting to the employees who rely on it, is costly. Hence, many organizations have looked for other alternatives.

These alternatives could mean outsourcing the travel function, or moving toward a self-service vehicle hosted on the organizations intranet site. While the outsourcing could mean turning to a traditional travel agent, this rarely happens. More likely, the company moves to a service such as the one developed by Expedia or one of the corporate booking portals.

As you read through the next page or two, you may find little to differentiate some of the services. To compete with services offered by organizations like Expedia, some of the airline sites, discussed in the section entitled Third-Party Corporate Booking Portals, are starting to display airfares offered by competitors. They have to or they will lose business to the more comprehensive sites run by companies like Expedia and Travelocity.

CORPORATE INTRANET PORTALS

A number of companies have created travel portals for their employees to use to arrange their travel. These typically are hosted on the corporate intranet site and can be accessed only through use of a user ID and password. Some are linked to the homepage that comes up on the employees' computers when they log in each morning.

These sites make it easy for employees to book travel and assist greatly in ensuring policy compliance. The self-service features make this an attractive option from a cost standpoint as there is no need for a large travel staff.

This area is rapidly evolving. These may be standalone sites or they may link into third-party service providers.

ONLINE CORPORATE BOOKING SERVICES

It will come as no surprise that the same dot-com giants (Expedia, Travelocity etc.) who changed the travel world by providing consumers with the same information that was once the province of travel agents have now turned their attention to the lucrative corporate travel market. These Internet newcomers are making their dent in the world of corporate travel. They tend to offer a complete suite of on-demand travel management tools and they service both large and small companies by helping them effectively manage their travel programs.

Once you register to use them, they will provide you with a suite of management reports to help you manage your programs. Here are two such sites:

1. www.expediacorporate.com
2. www.travelocitybusiness.com

THIRD-PARTY CORPORATE BOOKING PORTALS

Responding to the growing demand from corporate customers for direct access to their content, a number of airlines are redesigning their direct online corporate booking tool. These sites often bypass global distribution systems and some travel management firms to deliver to corporations the lowest price possible.

These portals claim to offer corporate travel managers new enhancements designed to make their job easier. Your travelers will like them not only because they are easy to use but because many offer bonus frequent-flyer miles when trips are booked through them. Some of the portals include some or all of the following features:

• Instant online access to real-time traveler data
• Improved reporting
• Easy integration into existing back-office systems

- Bonus mileage
- Reduced distribution costs
- Online refunds and exchanges
- Online and integrated reporting
- Ability to book multiple passengers
- Direct link to flight status notification
- Online seat selection
- Twenty-four-hour customer service support

Initially these portals were for a single airline. However, increased competition has forced some of them to include information about competitors' flights.

This is a highly volatile marketplace, with changes coming almost daily. The changes are increasing as airlines merge, go out of business, and purchase each other's routes. At this writing, here are a few of the portals that are up and running. Expect more in the near future:

> www.unitedgobusiness.com
> www.corporateaaccess.com
> www.continental.com/programs/btm/default.asp
> www.delta.com/business_programs_services/index.jsp
> www.jetblue.com/corporatetravel/companyblue.asp

Interestingly, these portals are targeting the mid-sized companies. They see real potential there. They allow employee self-service while providing the lowest cost. They are especially attractive to those organizations whose employees do much of their travel on one airline.

MAKING THE SELECTION: THIRD-PARTY TRAVEL SERVICE PROVIDER

Which is the best? There is no clear-cut answer. A lot will depend on what your requirements are, where you are located, and your corporate culture. If you are located in a city that is primarily serviced by one airline, there might be some advantage in going with the portal offered by that airline. However, given the business failures, the way airlines sell routes to each other or just give up on them, the emergence of new airlines, and a host of other issues, there would need to be a pretty compelling reason to sign up with one for a long time, although it does not appear that this is a requirement for these services.

The other advantage of some—but not all—of the single airline portals is that some provide your travelers with extra frequent-flyer points. While this may not be an advantage in some organizations, those looking to increase employee benefits without spending much money may find this is one way to do so.

The final decision may boil down to a serious evaluation of both the costs and the reporting available. Balancing the information you would like to have but are not getting from your existing T&E expense reporting module against the cost side of the equation will provide you with the answer—for today.

This is a rapidly changing arena. New services pop up regularly. So the analysis you do today may need to be redone in 6 to 12 months to ensure that there is not a better way for your organization.

BARE-BONES APPROACH: EMPLOYEE SELF-BOOKING

The Internet has put the latest travel information at the fingertips of virtually anyone who wants it. Consumers can get online and check flight and pricing information at any time of the day or night. In fact, it is this ability that sometimes leads to trouble for those organizations with substantial contracts with preferred suppliers. Their employees do a little surfing and find a rate better than the one offered by the preferred supplier on the particular route and day in question. And, they can do it in very little time.

Given the ease with which anyone with a modicum of Internet skills can book travel, a growing number of companies are requiring or allowing their employees to do just that. Employees are required to make their own reservations using one of the popular online sites or going directly to the airline's own web site.

The advantage of this approach to employees is that they get to select the exact flight they want, hopefully at a reasonable price.

DEMISE OF THE SATURDAY-NIGHT STAY AND OTHER COSTLY ISSUES

Not so long ago, in order to get a reasonable cost on an airline ticket, a Saturday-night stay was required. This often entailed negotiating between the employee and employer over the finances. Were the cost savings offset by the additional expense of another night in the hotel and meals? Was it fair to expect the employee to give up one or two days of his or her weekend? Should comp time be granted for those days?

For the most part, those requirements are gone. The only requirement that seems to affect airfares is the amount of time in advance that the reservation is made. Last-minute reservations are still costly, most of the time.

Even one-way tickets are available on some routes at a reasonable cost. Flying into one city and out of another no longer costs an arm and a leg on some routes. In fact, certain airlines (think JetBlue, Southwest, and so on) regularly sell tickets with each leg priced separately.

OTHER BOOKING ISSUES

Once you've traveled once or twice on company business you know it is no treat. Arriving home at two in the morning and having to be at work at eight the next morning is not exactly fair. But where do you draw the line? Here's a list of issues that should be addressed in the T&E policy. Otherwise you will end up with the employees in one department being treated very differently from employees in the next.

- *The red eye.* These are flights that typically leave late in the evening from the West Coast and arrive on the East Coast the next morning. The time difference combined with the flight time might put an employee on the ground in time to get to work the next day. If this is applicable to your organization, your policy should clearly state:
  - Whether employees are required to take such flights.
  - If they are required to take them, whether they are required to come to the office on the day of their return.
- *Comp days for company business.* If company business requires that an employee either travel or be involved in a meeting on a Saturday, Sunday, or holiday, will the employee be given a compensating day off?
- *Next day off after a late return home.* If an employee arrives home after a certain hour, can he take the next day off? Can he simply come in a few hours late? Whatever the decision, the times should be spelled out to avoid any misconceptions. If you just use the word *late*, the employee might interpret that to mean 9:00 P.M., while his boss might interpret that as midnight. This is an issue that may require some coordination with Human Resources. Keep in mind that airlines have trouble and an employee

who should have made it home by 9:00 might in actuality not arrive home until well after midnight.

- *Stopovers.* Are employees allowed to demand direct flights when a much less expensive alternative is available with a stopover? The policy should address this issue.
- *Early flights.* Are employees expected to take flights at six or seven in the morning if it will get them to their location in time for an early morning meeting or event or may they travel the day before and stay in a hotel paid for by the company? Can this choice be left to employees' own discretion, as some would prefer to stay at home with their families as much as possible while others prefer to avoid the wear and tear of getting to the airport for a 6:00 A.M. flight?
- *Costly hotels.* Some organizations have dollar limits on the hotel rates for their employees. Typically these rates are set by city. While this is not a completely unreasonable approach, it can backfire in certain circumstances. If employees are attending a conference, most of the conference attendees will stay at the hotel where the conference is being held, that is, assuming that several hotels are not being used. In the latter case, the employees then need to either take a cab back and forth from a hotel in the approved price range or rent a car and possibly pay for parking. Similar circumstances could arise when visiting a client whose office is in an expensive part of town. Common sense should rule. This might be an example of where a policy exemption should apply. This should be put in writing before the trip. How you wish to address such cases should be delineated in the policy.

These are just a few of the booking issues that can lead to problems. While it might be nice to rely on your employees' common sense and not to have to address each of these petty matters, that is not a great idea. History has shown that a few employees will be severely lacking in that area and another few will use any loophole they can to spend company money in ways not intended or worse.

3

T&E EXPENSE REPORT APPROVAL PROCESS

INTRODUCTION

The approval of travel and entertainment (T&E) expenses happens most frequently after the fact, if at all. Most organizations have moved away from pretrip approvals with few consequences. The thinking is that it would be almost impossible for an employee to plan and take a trip without the superior's approval. And if the employee were foolish enough to do such a thing, it would be an issue only in those organizations that provided the employee with a credit card with corporate liability. For if an employee took a trip without approval and put it on his or her credit card, the company would have no liability. While fraud is an issue for some organizations, this type of situation has rarely arisen. Hence, the formal approval process starts after the fact for most organizations.

WHO'S WATCHING THE STORE?

The other issue you may have noted is that we said that approvals are after the fact, if at all. The "if at all" refers to the fact that many managers across all sorts of organizations do not review their subordinates' T&E expense reports despite the fact that they sign their approval on them. This is an issue as it gives the employee the idea that no one is watching the store and puts the burden on Accounts Payable to ensure T&E policy compliance for the organization. This is discussed in detail in Chapter 10.

This is something, especially in light of Sarbanes-Oxley, that organizations need to change. The manager who approves an expense report with an obviously fraudulent expense or one that clearly violates company policy should be held just as accountable as the employee who made the expenditure. With that kind of responsibility, managers would pay more attention to this task.

APPROVAL PROCESS IN A PAPER WORLD

Whether an organization is using a paper form filled out in pen and ink or an online form based on Excel that needs to be printed and signed, the process is considered paper based for the purpose of this discussion. After completing the report the employee then attaches all his or her receipts and sends the entire package to his or her supervisor for approval.

After thoroughly reviewing the packet to ensure that everything is correct and as the manager had intended, the manager signs the T&E form and does one of two things. The report is either (1) returned to the employee, who is responsible for getting it to Accounts Payable for processing and reimbursement, or (2) sent straight to Accounts Payable for processing.

If a cash advance was involved in the trip and was not completely used or if the employee put some personal purchases on the company card (if this is allowed), the report should be accompanied by a personal check for the amount owed the organization.

As discussed earlier, unfortunately many managers do not review the packet and simply approve the report. Contrast this with the few rare managers who nitpick over every last dollar spent, delaying the processing and sometimes causing a delay that results in the employee having to pay the credit card bill out of his or her own pocket.

Problems can be caused if a supervisor is out for an extended period on business or vacation. A table of escalations should be drawn up so no employee is ever put in a position of having no one to approve his or her expense report before a credit card bill is due. Obviously, if the company pays the credit card bill this issue becomes of less import.

Employees who are concerned about getting their reimbursement can monitor this issue and should gently remind their superiors about it if the supervisor has not approved the report in a timely manner. Allowing several days for approval is not unreasonable.

TRAVELER OR SUPERVISOR: WHO SHOULD RETURN THE APPROVED FORM?

There are advantages and disadvantages to both processes. From a control standpoint it might be preferable to have the approver send the approved expense report to Accounts Payable for review and possible reimbursement. This decreases the likelihood that the employee will play games with the report. Consider, especially when using a handwritten form, how easy it would be for an employee to insert a 1 or 2 in front of a number, changing a $25 dinner into a $125 one, especially if dubious receipts were being used.

However, if the supervisors are not prompt in approving the expense reports and getting them sent off to Accounts Payable for processing, there is a real advantage in having the traveler involved. If the report goes back to the traveler and then on to Accounts Payable, the traveler will know when to remind his supervisor that the report needs to be approved and sent along. Of course, how high on the traveler's radar this issue remains is another consideration.

The reality after reviewing these factors, especially in light of Sarbanes-Oxley and with an eye to fraud prevention, is that it is a better control point to have the expense reports sent from the supervisor to Accounts Payable for processing. This issue is almost completely eliminated in the electronic process, as you will see from the ensuing discussion.

APPROVALS IN AN ELECTRONIC PROCESS

In the electronic world, the employee completes the report online and it is either sent to the supervisor for approval or sent to Accounts Payable for processing.

Yes, it can be sent without the supervisor's approval, if that is how the organization chooses to handle its T&E expense processing.

ELECTRONIC PROCESSING WITHOUT IMMEDIATE APPROVAL

The reason to send it without an approval is to get the bill from the credit card company paid in a timely manner. When this approach is used, supervisors get periodic reports for their review showing the T&E spend for their groups. These reports can be weekly or monthly depending on the volume and the wishes of the organization.

The supervisor who receives the report is expected to review the entire thing and he or she usually does. The advantage of this approach is that it is not sporadic and allows the supervisor to review all T&E expenditures in one sitting. It also puts the expenses into a larger framework. In this approach the supervisor has a tight time period in which to approve or question all expenses. If he or she does not respond within the allotted timeframe, the approval is escalated to his or her superior. From a career standpoint, this is not a good thing, and most managers will respond if for no other reason than to avoid dragging their boss into this equation.

ELECTRONIC PROCESSING WITH IMMEDIATE APPROVAL

It is more common, however, to get the manager's approval on the expenditure prior to sending the expense report to Accounts Payable for processing and reimbursement. If the report is finished online, it can be handled in one of two ways:

1. Forwarding it electronically to the manager
2. Forwarding a note with a link to the manager

The manager can then review the items and approve them online. When the approval is completed the authorization is sent either automatically or by e-mail to Accounts Payable, letting the staff there know that they can process the expense report. The authorization can trigger the notification to Accounts Payable. If there is a problem, the supervisor contacts the employee to discuss the issue.

With this automated approach, the employee should receive an automatic notification that the report has been approved and sent on for processing. Thus, if the employee has not received this notification, he or she can remind the supervisor to review the report.

This approach may or may not have the automated escalation feature described earlier. If it does, the odds of getting the report approved in a timely manner increase greatly.

APPROVALS: PAPER VERSUS ELECTRONIC

There is one area where paper reports have a big advantage. In many organizations, especially with considerate managers, the supervisor will approve the report the moment the employee brings it in for approval. There is no waiting and the issue of approvers sitting on reports delaying the process disappears.

However, that can be a problem. Have you seen it? These are the managers most likely to automatically approve the expense report without looking at anything on it. With the employee standing looking on, some managers are reluctant to pore over the report giving the impression that they do not trust the employee. And don't think that deceitful employees won't take advantage of this.

Clearly the electronic methodology is preferred. There is no need to worry about calculation errors, the expense report is legible, sometimes (depending on the approach used) automated policy compliance can be built into the process, and more. It is also the way of the future and it is only a matter of time before those handwritten reports go the way of the dinosaur completely.

SOMETHING TO CONSIDER

In most organizations, if a manager is out on vacation or company business, his or her supervisor will step in and approve reports along with other responsibilities. If the immediate manager will review reports thoroughly while his or her boss will sign anything, you may find employees holding their reports until their immediate supervisor is out of the office.

If such a pattern emerges, it should not be tolerated as it opens the door for that dishonest employee to steal from the company. Of course, the bottom line to this is no one should approve a report that he or she has not completely reviewed.

WHAT ABOUT THE RECEIPTS?

So far, we have not discussed how receipts are handled. The organization will decide at what level it needs receipts. In all cases it should be no higher than the IRS requirement. That is $75 in 2006. However, most organizations are still at the $25 level and some are even lower than that.

Traditionally, these were attached to the expense report before it was submitted for approval to be matched against the expense report when the report was received in Accounts Payable for processing. Some managers looked at them; most didn't.

The receipts are a real sore point in Accounts Payable. Some are barely legible, and some are huge pieces of paper while others are on tiny scraps of paper resembling adding machine tape. Needless to say, those tiny scraps of paper have a way of disappearing.

This has led to a number of innovations. The first was the requirement at certain companies that the traveler take all those little pieces of paper and tape them to an $8\frac{1}{2}$-by-11 piece of white paper. This got the receipts under some sort of control.

Some organizations, especially those with field locations, have arranged for a special fax number to be set up for use for submitting receipts. Each expense report is assigned its own unique tracking number (which is sometimes read as a bar code) and that number is used when sending the receipts into Accounts Payable via fax. The employees in these circumstances are supposed to either keep the original receipts themselves or put the original receipts in an envelope with the identifying number or bar code and send them into Accounts Payable.

Often Accounts Payable will not pay on the expense report until it has received the envelope containing the receipts. As you might imagine, this can turn into another issue. The employee completes the report but never manages to submit the receipts either because she has lost them or because it is too much of a clerical task and she forgets to do it.

Whatever the approach taken, the receipts need to be maintained and the correct procedure should be spelled out in the T&E policy manual.

INQUISITIVE MANAGERS AND RECEIPTS

You may have noted that except in the outdated paper-based process, there is no discussion of how the approver matches receipts to the report he is supposed to approve. Most of these processes eliminate that step. After all, if the manager is not going to review the report, what are the odds that he will match the receipts? This is a task that is done in Accounts Payable and is discussed in some detail elsewhere.

Regardless of the policy, you will run into a few managers who insist on seeing the receipts. Many are simply inquisitive but others want to do a thorough job in reviewing before approving. The reality is they are within their rights to request this information if they are to approve the expenditures. If they request to see the receipts, the employee should immediately share them. This means the employee really should not send original receipts to Accounts Payable until after the superior has approved the expense report. If the employee keeps the originals and sends in the copies or faxes in the receipts, then this will not be an issue.

4

THE T&E REVIEW
AND REIMBURSEMENT PROCESS

INTRODUCTION

Once the travel and entertainment (T&E) expense
report has been approved by the employee's supervisor and sent to Accounts Payable, the Accounts
Payable staff is responsible for reviewing the report
and reimbursing the employee for out-of-pocket
expenses. Depending on the organization's philosophy, the Accounts Payable group may also be
responsible for monitoring the expense report for
policy compliance.

The reimbursement function has another component in some
organizations. It is a prepayment option—the cash advance
feature.

CASH ADVANCES

Cash advances were originally designed to help financially overburdened traveling executives cover their company-related expenses that were put on personal credit cards. This was before corporate T&E cards became popular. These advances, once commonplace for traveling employees, are fast becoming a thing of the past in many (but not all) organizations. When employees pay for all their travel expenses themselves, these advances may be necessary, if other arrangements are not made. Other arrangements can be:

- A company credit card
- An allowance in the policy for the payment of tickets before the trip is taken
- A travel agency that arranges the trips and bills the company directly for air travel

Airline tickets, if booked sufficiently in advance to get lower rates, may have to be paid for weeks, if not months, in advance. Cash advances can lead to abuses. A few employees will request a much larger advance than they need. They often will put in for it far in advance of their trip, "just to be on the safe side."

What can they gain? If there are no limits on the cash advance and there is no interest charged on the cash advance loan, the employee may use the organization's money for his or her own purposes for several months.

This may have been more prevalent when interest rates were higher, but for cash-strapped employees the cash advance is still the way to go. This is not to say that all employees abused the cash advance system. Nothing could be farther from the truth.

Another issue affecting cash advances is that, in a very few cases, employees are tempted to fabricate expenses to justify not returning the cash.

OTHER CASH ADVANCE PROBLEM

Getting T&E expense reports turned in on time is an ongoing issue for those responsible for the process. It is not a problem with all traveling employees, but most organizations have a small contingent that just can't seem to get their reports turned in on time. This leads to a number of problems.

One of the benefits of having the employees be out of pocket for expenses is that they have a vested interest in getting their reports turned in on time in order to be reimbursed. They need the funds to pay their credit card bill. If the company has advanced the employee cash to cover these expenses, the employee no longer has that concern. For a few, this is enough to make them tardy in completing their reports.

HOW COMMON ARE CASH ADVANCES?

Less than half (47%) the companies responding to the *Accounts Payable Now & Tomorrow* survey indicated that their organizations offered cash advances. Even those who do offer them tend to do so on a limited or restricted basis. Also, having a T&E card and offering cash advances are not mutually exclusive. Some companies do both.

There's one other point to consider regarding these advances. There are supposed to be tax consequences to the recipient if the money is not accounted for within a reasonable amount of time. You might use this stick to entice T&E reimbursement reports from those who have outstanding cash advances and can't seem to find the time to get their reports done. For additional information on the tax issues, please refer to Chapter 5 on tax implications.

EXPENSE REIMBURSEMENT

Employee expense reimbursements can be handled in one of several ways. These include:

- Handing a check to the employee
- Mailing a check to the employee's house
- Including the reimbursement in the employee's paycheck
- Having the reimbursement direct deposited along with payroll
- Having the reimbursement direct deposited to a bank account

This seemingly innocuous task can create havoc in organizations that insist on using payroll-related reimbursements. A few employees use their T&E reimbursements as "mad money," not sharing this money with their spouse. These individuals may create an uproar if they are told to either have the reimbursement included in a paycheck or have the funds direct deposited to the account where the paycheck is deposited.

A best practice is to have the reimbursements direct deposited into a bank account. Most plans will allow the deposit into more than one account. Hence, the employee with the spouse issue can set up another bank account to handle the T&E funds, isolating it from the eyes of his or her employer. This meets the needs of both parties. Should the employee not be willing to do this, it is not the employer's responsibility to adjust its processes to accommodate the employee.

There is another reason to avoid the hand-delivery-of-check method of reimbursement. Aside from the obvious inefficiencies and costs associated with this approach, it is an internal controls issue. Any return of check to the requestor opens the door to fraud and or potential duplicate payments. Hence, returning checks by hand to employees should be avoided at all costs.

From a cost control standpoint, reimbursement should be through an automated clearinghouse (ACH) payment to employees' bank accounts. It does not matter whether it is the same account used for payroll or another. Of course, those organizations that choose to include expense reimbursement with payroll have closed off this option for their employees—and that is the employer's right.

LAST-MINUTE REIMBURSEMENTS: THE DEMANDING EMPLOYEE

On a regular basis, the Accounts Payable department has to deal with employees demanding their T&E reimbursement immediately. So, what's the Accounts Payable staff supposed to do when an employee is ranting and raving and demanding her reimbursement immediately even though she's missed all the cutoffs? This is a situation loaded with other implications. In addition to the financial issues already discussed, the employee could be hitting up against her credit limit. This can have ugly repercussions and impact the employee's family.

Recognizing these factors, the first issue is to make sure that the employees have their T&E report filled out completely and approved. If it is not approved, there is nothing Accounts Payable can do. The Accounts Payable department simply does not have the authority to issue a payment. Make this clear to the employees and suggest that the appropriate approval be obtained before they request reimbursement.

Assuming that the return has the appropriate signatures on it, you are effectively dealing with another Rush check situation.

The first thing you might want to ascertain is whether this is a one-time occurrence for the employee in question or this has happened numerous times before with this employee. If the answer is the latter, it is probably time to draw a line in the sand and stand firm—or the situation will never improve.

If, however, it is a one-time occurrence, you might want to be accommodating, and issue the check with the understanding that you won't do it again. There is one instance when you might have to be more flexible. Some managers sit on their employees' T&E reports for weeks on end. It's not fair to the employees but there is little they can do. In most organizations, these executives' reputation precedes them and you will know who they are. You might want to be a little more accommodating if this is the case.

Finally, as with any other Rush check scenario, there is one last point to consider. Don't refuse to issue a check to someone if you know they will go to your boss and you will be overridden.

By recognizing if your company's policies are contributing to the demanding employee reimbursement issue, you will have taken the first step in addressing the issue. Once you know where you stand, you can develop a policy to minimize the problems.

REVIEWING AND CHECKING T&E EXPENSE REPORTS

When the expense reports arrive in Accounts Payable approved for payment, in theory, Accounts Payable should simply be able to pay the report based on the employees' information and the managers' approval. The key words here are *in theory*.

As anyone who has been actively involved in T&E is painfully aware, a large percentage of managers will sign any report that one of their employees places in front of them without looking at anything on the report. They trust their employees. This is not a good thing. It means that there is no oversight on what is put on the report. And, don't think that employees who work for such managers are not aware that they can get away with murder on their T&E expense reports. A few will take advantage of this fact. And a few will make honest errors on their reports.

Hence, it is really a good idea to have Accounts Payable, or whoever is responsible for processing T&E, check for policy compliance. If your organization is one of those using an automated T&E system that has a policy-compliance module, and you have that module turned on, this will not be an issue for you. However, most readers of this book will not fall into that group.

In most organizations, Accounts Payable will and should check expense reports. But, how much checking is enough? After all, for the most part, T&E is not a large component of an organization's spend.

SPOT CHECKING

When it comes to verifying information on T&E reimbursement requests, finding a middle ground is not easy. If you are using one of those nifty models that does policy compliance along with other verifications, verifying 100% of the reports is generally overkill. As a best practice it is generally recommended that companies only spot check reports. But this is one area where recommended best practices and reality take a divergent road.

When *Accounts Payable Now & Tomorrow* asked its readers if they completely checked every detail of every report, a whopping 66.22% indicated that they did.

When companies that spot check their employees' T&E reimbursement requests were asked what they checked, the answers were all over the place. Here's what some of them indicated:

- Random 10% are completely checked.
- Every item over $500.
- Every out-of-policy item.
- Receipts are compared to what is charged on all claims over $1,000.
- More than we should have to.
- Random sampling.
- 20%; it's hard to check all details.
- Complete audit of 25% as well as selected individuals.
- 90%. (Author's comment: Why bother?)
- 80%. We check any receipt that exceeds $75 to verify that all receipts are provided and we check all executives.
- Check certain categories such as office supplies for unreimbursable items.
- 10%.
- The manager is supposed to check and sign the form before it is sent to Accounts Payable.
- We audit each individual using the expense report system at least once a year.
- It varies, but high spenders get more attention. Consistent problem reports are checked more often.
- New card holders are checked 100% for a while.
- 20% plus 100% of any red-flagged reports within the automated system.
- 1 to 2%.
- 80%.
- 30 to 40%; we have an atmosphere of trust.
- 10% and all over $1,000.
- 50 to 60%.

- 10% each month; if we believe that an associate has violated guidelines, that associate will be part of the 10%.
- 30% since our air/rail and company card gas are centrally billed—we do check all reports to make sure they are not expensing these.
- 90%—we don't check receipts less than $25.
- 80%—T&E system has audit rules based on dollar amount, expense type plus 10% random.
- We actually audit every fifth expense report that comes across the Accounts Payable clerks' desks.
- 50%—we verify everything over $500.

CHECKING: AN IMPORTANT CONSIDERATION

There is one important consideration that is often overlooked when checking T&E reimbursement requests and it has nothing to do with T&E but everything to do with the financial wherewithal of the organization. Employee fraud, as you may be aware, is most frequently committed by long-term, trusted employees. And crooks who get away with one theft can rarely resist the lure of another, especially when it seems so easy—like T&E fraud. More than one company has uncovered an ongoing fraud elsewhere in their organization because the crooked employee couldn't resist cheating on his or her T&E report.

This is not to imply that every company has employees who are crooks. That is far from the truth. However, when these employees get going they can do untold damage.

RECOMMENDED BEST PRACTICE: CHECKING REPORTS

Most experts come down heavily on the side of spot checking. Given the limited resources of most Accounts Payable departments, it is not a good use of talent to check every last detail. It's like spending a dollar to save a dime. True, some policy violations will get through, but in the scheme of things the dollar amount in question will be small. As a recommended best practice policy, you should check 5 to 10% of all reports plus all reports of employees who have had serious T&E issues in the past.

Additionally, once a year, identify several travelers (some randomly and some known to be problems) and pull their reports for the prior 14 months. Review all the reports together in detail. Occasionally you will find the same receipt used on multiple reports. By spanning more than one year, you will have a better chance of finding problems.

IF MANAGEMENT WON'T AGREE TO SPOT CHECKING

Interestingly, some usually progressive people are aghast at the thought of not checking every report thoroughly. I always find this amusing, but it is a fact of life as demonstrated by the statistics shown earlier. If you find yourself in this position, don't give up. Few companies really have the resources to check every detail on every report. Just start small.

Get management approval to spot check 90% of all reports plus any over $1,000. If they are dragging their heels, put this issue in reserve until the right time presents itself. That right time might be if there are to be staff layoffs or perhaps your department is asked to take on additional work without increasing staff. Bring this issue up again at that time.

Once you get started, realize that you have a way to go. After everyone is comfortable with your small program, raise the ante. If you started checking 90%, try moving it down to 75%. If that seems like to big a jump for your management team, go for 80%. However, if your corporate culture is one where all it takes is a small success for management to get on board, go for 50%. You get the idea.

WHEN SPOT CHECKING MAY NOT BE APPROPRIATE

One Accounts Payable manager I know at a particularly progressive company reported that in his Accounts Payable department they checked 100% of all expense reports turned in. I was a bit surprised, given how progressive this large financial institution was in everything else it did in Accounts Payable, so I asked the manager why.

His answer was quite simple. In his company most of the traveling and entertaining was done by high-flying traders. These were people who traded in million-dollar increments all day. To them, $500 was a rounding issue, not something to be investigated. In fact, the same could probably be said for $50,000. Hence the expense reports that came in from this group would make even the most liberal managers' hair stand straight up. For groups like this, 100% verification might be a good thing.

POLICY COMPLIANCE

Checking for policy compliance and then taking action when an employee is out of compliance with the T&E policy is not an easy task. Unless you are using one of those automated systems, this is a review that needs to be done manually. How noncompliance is handled will vary from organization to organization. Clearly someone who has spent $5 over the allowable limit for a meal should not be treated in the same manner as someone who has taken his girlfriend out for dinner on a Saturday night and charged it on the company credit card.

In general, an employee who has put through some minor item that is out of compliance with the company policy should be given the opportunity to remove the expense from his or her report with no further repercussions. However, if there is blatant abuse or worse, the superior of the approving manager should be notified. Needless to say, the employee should not be reimbursed for the noncompliant items.

By holding the approving manager equally responsible with the employee submitting the abusive or fraudulent expenses, organizations put back a level of review and oversight that is missing in many cases. The fact that the manager did not take the time to review an expense report before approving it should not be an acceptable excuse. If the manager is not willing to perform the task correctly, it should be given to someone who will.

Some common sense needs to apply. Several years ago there was a published story of a traveling employee whose company limited him to $10 for breakfast. The hotel he was staying in charged $12 for breakfast. This scheming employee took a cab to a restaurant that offered a breakfast within his expense restraints and then another back to the hotel where his conference was being held. He spent the allowed $10 for breakfast and another $25 for taxicab rides, which had no limits. He was proud enough of his "accomplishment" to brag about it to a reporter, but bright enough to do it anonymously.

The only time it is recommended that you check expense reports in enough detail to uncover such manipulations is if fraud is suspected. Otherwise you are spending the proverbial dollar to save a dime. It's just not an effective use of your employees' time.

POLICY COMPLIANCE EXCEPTIONS

As noted above, there are times when exceptions to the company T&E policy may be approved. Ideally, these will be in advance (e.g., if the preferred air supplier offers only a few, poorly timed flights to the location the traveler needs to visit.) Any approved exceptions should be noted in writing and the documentation for that exception should be:

- Maintained by the traveler
- Submitted along with the expense report, if the process allows, along with all other receipts

This will help avoid problems down the road when everyone has long forgotten the trip and that the policy exception was approved.

5

ACCOUNTABLE OR NOT: THE TAX IMPLICATIONS OF YOUR T&E PLAN

INTRODUCTION

There is a silver lining buried deep in the tax code. As you might imagine, the IRS has a lot to say about what can and cannot be deducted by companies on their income tax returns. This is especially true when it comes to T&E and, yes, we are going to discuss this in some detail. The silver lining is that these requirements can be used as a carrot to get employees to do what they are supposed to do (i.e., turn their expense reimbursement requests in on a timely basis), or there are some negative repercussions from a tax standpoint. The employee could end up with additional taxable income if some of the rules are not followed.

AN ACCOUNTABLE PLAN

The key here is what's referred to as an *accountable plan*. To be an accountable plan, the company's reimbursement or allowance arrangement must include all three of the following rules:

1. The expenses must have a business connection; that is, the employee must have paid or incurred deductible expenses while performing services as an employee of the employer.
2. The employee must adequately account to the employer for these expenses within a reasonable period of time.
3. The employee must return any excess reimbursement or allowance within a reasonable period of time.

Needless to say, this definition raises more questions than it answers.

REASONABLE AMOUNT OF TIME

The innocuous words, *reasonable amount of time*, are the afore-mentioned carrot. Here's why. Although the definition of a reasonable amount of time is not set in stone, this is what most companies consider reasonable:

- Employees must account for their expenses within 60 days of when the expenses were incurred.
- Employees must return any excess reimbursement (cash advances) within 120 days after the expense was paid or incurred.

TAX IMPLICATIONS OF AN ACCOUNTABLE PLAN

Very simply, if an accountable plan is in place, companies do not have to include T&E reimbursements on their employees' W-2 forms and employees do not have to pay income tax on these funds. Needless to say, from the employees' point of view, this is the preferred approach and is the one used by most organizations.

A NONACCOUNTABLE PLAN

A plan that does not meet all three of the guidelines presented earlier in the description of an accountable plan is considered a nonaccountable plan. In this case, the company must include any reimbursements or expense allowances paid to employees with their wages and report them on Form W-2 as income.

Under these circumstances, employees may deduct the expenses on their own expense reports but are subject to:

• The 50% deduction limit on meals and entertainment
• The 2% adjustment for total expenses that applies to miscellaneous itemized deductions

Additionally, the employee is responsible for the paperwork and any taxes owed on amounts that are not deductible as explained earlier.

ADVANTAGES OF AN ACCOUNTABLE PLAN

Clearly it is to the employees' advantage to be covered under an accountable plan. But the employee is not the only one who benefits.

If you report the expenses as wages your company will be required to pay the employer's portion of FICA taxes on this money. That effectively increases the company's cost of

T&E. Additionally, you will be required to withhold the appropriate taxes.

There is no requirement that the plan be accountable or nonaccountable, but it appears to be in both parties' best financial interest to have an accountable plan. You might remind your employees of their financial interest if you are having trouble getting them to turn in expense reimbursement reports.

TAX CARROT/STICK

If employees don't conform to these guidelines, their companies can threaten tax action. That's right; if accounting and return of excess reimbursement are not done within a reasonable amount of time, the employee has effectively turned the plan into a nonaccountable plan for himself or herself.

If that happens, the company is required to report this money as income to the employee on his or her W-9. The employee will then be liable for the income tax as if it were income.

RECEIPTS UNDER ACCOUNTABLE PLANS

The IRS requirement for receipts is that receipts are required for all expenditures in excess of $75. However, most companies have more stringent requirements and are still stuck at the $25 level.

Additionally, it is necessary to obtain the hotel folio when your employees travel. It is not sufficient to simply have the credit card receipt. This is because meals are often charged to the hotel room and these are not 100% deductible.

T&E IN A PAPERLESS WORLD

You may be wondering whether you need to save all your employees' receipts and paperwork related to T&E for tax purposes. According to ruling Revenue Procedure 97-22, the IRS allows one to prepare, record, transfer, index, store, preserve, retrieve, and reproduce books and records by either electronically imaging hardcopy documents to an electronic storage medium, or transferring computerized books and records to an electronic storage medium that allows them to be viewed or reproduced without using the original program.

This means that you may destroy the original hardcopy books and records and delete the original computerized records after a taxpayer completes testing of the storage system. The electronic records then become the official legal records.

PERTINENT IRS PUBLICATIONS

If you have any questions about IRS regulations related to T&E, refer to the following publications:

- IRS Publication 463 focuses on rules and regulations related to travel, entertainment, and gifts: http://www.irs. gov/pub/irs-pdf/p463.pdf.
- IRS Publication 535 explains common business expenses and explains what is and is not deductible: http://www.irs. gov/pub/irs-pdf/p535.pdf.
- Revenue Procedure 97-22 regulations on electronic storage.

ANOTHER REASON TO ELIMINATE CASH ADVANCES

Aside from the obvious issues discussed elsewhere throughout this book, there is another reason to avoid cash advances. If you have an accountable plan, which most companies do, there are concerns with employees who receive cash advances but do not return the excess within 120 days of their travel. You run the risk of having your plan lose its accountable plan status if cash advance excesses are not returned within 120 days of the employee travel. If you have this problem on a regular basis, you might want to discuss it with your tax advisor.

Additionally, you might consider revoking the cash advance privileges of any employee who abuses this feature. While this might seem a bit harsh, the employee's actions are jeopardizing the entire plan.

NEW TAX RULES: PER DIEMS *MAY* BE TAXABLE

On November 9, 2006, the IRS issued a new ruling which changes the way organizations must treat per-diems under certain conditions. The ruling was effective immediately although recognizing that it might take a little time for organizations to make the change, the IRS instructed its agents not to apply the revenue ruling for taxable periods ending on or before Dec. 31, 2006, in the absence of intentional noncompliance. After that everyone must comply.

If an employer routinely pays per diem allowances in excess of the federal per diem rates, and does not:

- track the allowances,
- require the employees either to actually substantiate all the expenses or pay back the excess amounts, and
- include the excess amounts in the employee's income and wages,

then the entire amount of the expense allowances is subject to income tax and employment tax.

6

PAYING FOR CORPORATE TRAVEL:
T&E CARDS

INTRODUCTION

Paying employees' travel bills can be a chore. The expenses are almost always in excess of $100 and often in excess of $1,000. No one in their right mind would expect the employees to walk around with that kind of cash in their pockets. Hence most of these expenses are put on credit cards. The credit card mechanism can work in any one of the following ways:

- The employee's own credit card with the employee completely responsible for obtaining the credit card and paying the bill.
- A company T&E card with the employee responsible for paying the bill.

- A company T&E card with the employee responsible for paying the bill but the company guaranteeing the payment and making payment should the employee default.
- A company T&E card with the company paying the bill.
- T&E purchases being combined with a corporate p-card (purchasing card) program and on one card, interestingly enough referred to as a *one card*. (Fuel payments are also included on these cards, if the organization has a fuel program.)
- The employee responsible for all payments, either through his or her own credit card or a company T&E card, but airfares paid for by the company on a corporate bill.

Each approach has advantages and disadvantages.

EMPLOYEE USE OF OWN CREDIT CARD

Many employees like to use their own credit cards because they rack up frequent-flyer miles or other goodies based on the dollar amounts put on the cards. Of course, if this is the employee's motivation, he or she might be tempted to charge something that is not actually needed.

Some question whether it is fair to expect employees to use their own credit for the benefit of the company. Also, employees with limited credit availability might end up strapped for personal expenditures if they have used their credit for the company.

Finally, some employees, either because they are young and have not established credit or have had problems with credit in the past, may not be able to get cards. The company, if it wishes these employees to travel, will need to make arrangements for them. Of course, this puts these employees in the embarrassing position of having to share their personal finances with their employer.

And, it is this situation that leads to those stressful confrontations between employees who have forgotten to submit their T&E expense report in a timely manner and Accounts Payable when the employee's credit card bill becomes due. The employee expects Accounts Payable to drop everything and get the reimbursement check prepared and Accounts Payable has its own priorities—and helping employees who have created their own problems is not one of them.

There is another issue with the use of a personal credit card. It provides deceitful employees with a mechanism to defraud their companies. Because they can charge and receive refunds for many things on the card, the employer has to check certain things extra thoroughly. For example, if the employee took a less expensive flight than he put in for, use of a personal card or cards would provide the flexibility to play all sorts of games.

The easy way around this issue is to require that employees turn in credit card bills for every month if they use the card for business expenses. But, this smacks of Big Brother and also of an invasion of privacy that most companies would prefer to avoid. To be perfectly honest, the few times I have used a personal credit card to pay for a business item, I have blacked out everything else on the bill.

Your employees may from time to time be forced to use their personal credit cards if the enterprise they are purchasing from does not take the card in question. Some places won't take American Express while others will take only American

Express. The same is true for MasterCard and VISA. While this is becoming less of an issue, it still occurs from time to time.

COMPANY CARD WITH EMPLOYEE PAYING THE BILL

This situation is a lot like the prior one, only the employee usually doesn't get the benefit of the frequent-flyer points. However, the employee also doesn't have his or her own credit on the line, which is generally a plus for the employee.

Generally, the banks that provide cards in these situations will do a credit check on the employee. If the employee meets their standards they will issue the card. If not, the matter then boils down to whether the company is willing to guarantee the payment. In this situation, most companies step up to the plate.

Unfortunately, this arrangement still results in confrontations when the employee has forgotten to turn in his or her expense report in time to get the reimbursement needed to pay the credit card bill.

Whether the employee is permitted to put personal charges on company cards is a question that needs to be addressed in the T&E policy. Some companies allow it and others don't. Most will tolerate it on occasion in case of emergency, as long as the employee brings it to their attention immediately after the use. It's when the employee "forgets" that problems arise.

Although it is generally a good idea to discourage employees from putting personal charges on these cards, some companies have no problem with it.

COMPANY CARD, EMPLOYEE PAYMENT, CORPORATE GUARANTEE

This situation is much like the previous one, except that the credit situation of the employee is not an issue. The company is required to make payment on any card where an employee has defaulted.

When this corporate guarantee is in place, the issue of learning when an employee has been terminated is especially important. A disgruntled employee in rare circumstances will take the card and go on a spending spree. Getting reimbursed for those funds can be next to impossible.

Those companies that have cards with corporate guarantees should work closely with Human Resources to ensure they are notified immediately of any terminations. That way the cards can be canceled immediately.

COMPANY PAYING THE T&E CARD BILL

While the company paying the bill might be great for the employee, it does tend to encourage poor behavior when it comes to filling out and turning in T&E expense reports after trips. The bottom line is the employee has no real incentive to complete this often-onerous task. There is no credit card bill waiting to be paid.

From the banks' standpoint, there is no credit issue as it is the organization's credit and not the individual's that determines whether a card will be issued.

From a corporate prospective, if the corporate culture is nurturing and protective, this might be the approach the organization chooses to take.

Finally, there are the same issues regarding departing employees as when there is a corporate guarantee. Accounts payable needs to be notified and the cards canceled immediately any time any cardholder departs—be it from choice or by invitation.

ONE CARD APPROACH

Frankly, we expect to see this approach become more popular with all organizations that have active purchasing card programs.

What used to be a much whispered about secret is now out in the open. Credit card companies offer rebates to their corporate clients who use their cards for significant volume. When this approach was started, companies needed a monthly volume of at least $500,000 to qualify.

I have recently heard of card issuers who will give rebates to organizations charging $50,000 on average. This is one of the few ways that Accounts Payable can generate some revenue for their organizations, because let's face it, generally speaking Accounts Payable is a cost center. So, those who are aggressively pursuing that rebate look for ways to increase the spend on the card. It didn't take them long to turn their eyes toward their spending on T&E. For many companies, this was a no-brainer way to get a larger rebate.

Thus was born the one card. Those with fuel programs started putting their fuel purchases on this one card instead of their fuel cards. This is effectively the same as the cards discussed previously: the corporate pay T&E card. It has all the benefits for the employees and can lead to some of the same headaches, namely the employee who is forgetful about turning in his or her expense report because there are no personal consequences for not turning them in.

HYBRID APPROACH

Employees using their own cards or company cards but paying the bill themselves sometimes run into a hitch. Airline tickets often must be purchased weeks if not months in advance in order to secure reservations and get the best rate. Yet, the employee usually cannot be reimbursed for these expenses until after the trip.

Especially if international travel is involved, it is an unfair burden on the employee to expect the employee to be out of pocket for months at a time for airfare for company travel. Thus, many organizations that use one of the approaches that entail the employee being responsible for the bill will handle travel separately. The employee will make the reservations using whatever method the employer designates (see Chapter 2), but the payment for the airline ticket will be billed directly to the company. The employee will still be expected to turn in boarding passes to verify his or her travel but will not have to deal with paying for the airline ticket.

This approach also provides information that can be used to track unused tickets and ensure that the company either gets a refund or uses the credits for those tickets on future purchases.

WHICH APPROACH IS BEST?

There is no simple answer to this question. As can be seen from the discussion so far, each approach has some benefits and some drawbacks. To a large extent the selection will boil down to corporate culture. Some organizations would not think of asking their employees to pay the credit card bills associated with their corporate travel while others would not dream of giving employees a corporate card.

Whichever approach is taken, the requirements should be spelled out in the policy and steps taken to protect the organization if the company credit is on the line.

ISSUANCE OF COMPANY T&E CARDS

In most instances employees must use their own cards. That's because over half (53.52%) of the companies responding to an *Accounts Payable Now & Tomorrow* survey indicated that they don't give employees a T&E card.

Even if the company does provide the card, the employee isn't off the hook. At slightly over half (58%) of the companies issuing cards, the company makes the payment. As you can see in the following table, responsibility for payment still resides with the employee at 42% of the companies that offer cards:

The employce	29%
The employee, but the company must pay if the employee defaults	13%
The company	58%

The numbers demonstrate that at least for the foreseeable future, Accounts Payable groups everywhere will continue to deal with employees who need their reimbursement for the credit card bill and who need it quickly.

7

RECEIPTS, DOCUMENTATION, AND OTHER ISSUES

INTRODUCTION

The very nature of reimbursement made for expenses incurred while on company business leads to some dispute. While one employee may feel that a bottle of wine with dinner is standard, the next may not. The problem arises when the employee who feels entitled to that bottle of wine works for the one who sees it as a luxury. This is just the tip of the iceberg when it comes to issues that are likely to cause dispute if employees are left to their own discretion when it comes to such spending.

This is why spelling out what the company will and will not do in the T&E policy and procedures manual is so strongly recommended. It avoids the no-one-ever-told-me or I-didn't-know type of excuses, or my favorite, "At my other company we were allowed to..." It's amazing what other companies will allow when there is no one available to refute the claims, which seem to grow in their ridiculousness the longer an employee has been with your organization. In this chapter we'll address a few of the issues that tend to cause the most trouble for organizations.

PER DIEMS

This Latin phrase, whose literal translation means *per day*, is typically used to describe the specific amount of money an organization allows an individual to spend per day when traveling on company business. It is usually used to cover meals and incidentals. Most U.S. companies and organizations use the per diem rate guide published by the General Services Administration (GSA).

The rates are updated typically once a year, although this may be more frequent if there is some good external reason. Sample rates for 2006 are shown in Appendix A. The rates vary by city. If you use the per diem approach, based on GSA numbers, in your travel and expense processes, expect to get a lot of complaints. Your employees will swear that it is impossible to get by on the amounts of money offered.

RECEIPTS

IRS guidelines require receipts for expenditures in excess of $75. However, most companies find this level a little high and require that employees submit receipts for expenditures in excess of $25. Still others require a receipt for everything. You will find that, whatever dollar limit you set for receipts, you will have an amazing number of expenses just under that dollar amount.

The other issue regarding receipts is how they are sent to Accounts Payable. This issue is discussed in some detail in

Chapter 3. Traditionally, receipts were attached to the expense report. Small pieces of paper of differing sizes cause problems. To get these small pieces of paper under control, some companies insist that these receipts be taped to a piece of paper before they are submitted. You may or may not require your employees to do this. While some prefer to get receipts in this method, others hate it.

At some companies, receipts are submitted along with the report so the approver can verify that the expenses are accurate. Then the receipts are shipped along with the report to Accounts Payable. Another approach is to have the receipts sent in a barcoded envelope for filing. Companies that utilize electronic T&E approaches typically employ this approach.

WHAT ABOUT ELECTRONIC RECEIPTS?

The IRS recently indicated that it will accept electronic data as documentation for corporate T&E expenses charged to corporate cards that meet given security requirements. Data from T&E card vendors that exercise reasonable controls to ensure integrity, accuracy, and reliability of the data, and to protect data from additions, alterations, or deletions, will probably be considered an acceptable alternative to paper receipts.

Your decision will depend on your policy. Do you want the paper receipts or are you comfortable with the electronic process? If you are comfortable with the electronic process, make sure that your card issuer meets the IRS guidelines.

Some companies look to ensure tighter controls by relying on the electronic receipts for recordkeeping purposes and mandating that their employees turn in the paper receipts for monitoring purposes.

In any event, hotel folios need to be turned in. This detail is needed for tax reporting purposes as many employees routinely charge their meals to their hotel rooms when traveling. It is also the way to discover whether an employee has charged a movie, or some other item not covered per your policy to his or her room.

DISASTER RECOVERY: LESSONS LEARNED FROM CHARLIE AND KATRINA

When the topic of business travel and entertainment is discussed, most of the focus is on conferences and business trips. But there is another side to T&E, and that is when something goes wrong. Disaster recovery is a topic that often gets short shrift in travel and entertainment discussions. It's not that the professionals who work in the function think it's not important; they simply can't get the necessary management focus. All that changes when there is a T&E card or corporate credit card program and there is a disaster. More to the point, the issue gets top-line attention when the cards are used by emergency personnel like employees of the local power and gas company. Clearly, when sending employees out in emergency situations, corporate T&E cards play a key role in how their requirements are met.

As everyone reading this is aware, Florida has had its share of emergencies in the last year or two, all courtesy of Mother Nature. The following advice was offered by several speakers at the National Association of Purchasing Card Professionals' recent annual forum. The speakers pointed out that in Florida, where they are based, they have an added advantage of other disasters. The advantage, if you will, is that there is some warning before hurricanes hit. Usually, it is possible to predict when and where a hurricane will hit, so some planning is possible.

Based on hard-earned experience, they recommend the following:

- No-name cards can be a problem. These cards generally are inactive and will need to be activated. While this can be done, it certainly adds to the stress of the situation and depending on electrical and phone capabilities can be a problem.
- The Merchant Category Codes (MCC) on cards designed as emergency cards can be modified quickly to allow for purchases in categories normally restricted. This might include food and hotels.
- Ideally, employees should have to rely on only one piece of plastic. This should be their regular card, perhaps with MCC restrictions lifted, as mentioned above.
- Consider seasonal raises in limits, especially in areas that have seasonal problems such as hurricanes or excessive snow. In any event, make it very easy to raise the limits on cards used by employees likely to be involved in disaster recovery.
- Do not use online travel reservation services in times of disaster recovery. Call the local hotels yourself.
- Be aware that getting rooms can be difficult as there will be a number of companies competing for the same rooms. Remember, if it is a natural disaster, FEMA, insurance companies, and various government agencies are all likely to be jockeying for rooms.
- Reserve a block of rooms in the locations you are likely to need them.
- P-cards or at a minimum corporate travel cards are a necessity. Without them, getting necessary supplies is likely to be difficult. At a time like this, vendors do not want your purchase orders.
- If there is no power, do not despair. Your p-cards and corporate credit cards will still hold the day. The vendors

will resort to the old way: writing information on paper and running the information through later, at which time you will get your receipt.

- Review periodically to make sure that the right people have cards, that is, those people who will be out in the field doing the work.

- Although documentation is the last thing on anyone's mind in times of disaster, if at all possible, employees should be directed to get the necessary receipts for their expenditures. Otherwise, afterward, if reimbursement from FEMA or other government agencies is required, it could be difficult without proper documentation.

OTHER DELICATE ISSUES

There are a number of matters that are a big deal in some organizations and of no concern to others:

- Liquor
- Movies
- Spouses

Liquor

Depending on your organization, this may not be an issue. However, for some it is a serious matter and the policy strictly forbids payment for alcohol. Some go so far as to require that the employee submit the detailed bill that shows what was ordered. In these instances, employees are advised to request a separate bill for the liquor. The idea is that the liquor is paid for with personal funds. If the policy is strict, this can be true even for a bottle of beer or glass of wine.

There is no right or wrong answer for this. It is simply a matter of policy and as long as it is spelled out in the policy manual given to employees there should be no problem.

Movies

Few companies will pay for movies that their employees watch while on company business. Checking the hotel folio is also the way to discover whether an employee has charged a movie to his or her room. If your policy does not cover movies, and most don't, you will need to have the employee reimburse you for this. While hotels are capable of preparing two bills for a stay and segregating charges at the employee's direction, it takes a lot of work and time, especially when the employee is trying to check out of the hotel quickly.

Thus, most will leave the movie on the company bill and simply reimburse the firm. Many companies choose to look the other way on this issue as the dollar amount is small and the annoyance associated with trying to straighten it out is not worth the effort. It should be noted that many companies are silent on this issue and while they may say they won't pay, they do. One can only hope that the employees use some common sense and discretion in their selection of entertainment.

Spouses

Most organizations will not pay for spousal travel unless the spouse of the traveling employee is actively participating in company business. The tax regulations address this issue, as more than one high-powered executive has discovered the hard way. However, if there is no additional charge for a second person staying in the room—and there rarely is—few organizations object to a spouse (or child or friend) accompanying the traveler.

8

COMMUNICATING REQUIREMENTS: THE T&E POLICY AND MANUAL

INTRODUCTION

Most organizations, but not all, publish a travel and entertainment (T&E) manual that delineates their corporate travel and entertainment policy and instructs their employees on their rules and regulations. This policy is the starting point for the administration of T&E expenditures and reimbursements within the company.

WHAT KIND OF POLICY DO YOU WANT?

Your T&E policy and the accompanying manual that describes the policy to your employees provide the framework for how the policy will be administered. How much discretion is allowed is a function of the level of detail in the policy. This is a corporate decision.

Some organizations have policies that run almost 100 pages, laying the ground rules for every possible action. The advantage

71

of this is there can be no question as to how things are done and what is covered. The disadvantage to such a policy is that few employees will take the time to read it if it is too long.

Some organizations go the opposite route, publishing rather short policies. This increases the likelihood that employees will read the policy but opens the door to individual interpretation—and that can backfire.

Additionally, short policies result in different managers making different rules for their employees. For example, the sales manager might interpret the policy quite loosely, while an accounting manager might require his or her employees to be more frugal in their spending while on company business.

There is no right or wrong answer to this question. It is a matter of corporate policy and one that needs to be addressed at the highest levels. However, if you are a public company you might have to consider the internal controls issue.

YOUR T&E POLICY, INTERNAL CONTROLS, AND THE SARBANES-OXLEY ACT

While your corporate culture might dictate a T&E policy that is loose and without too many restrictions, if your company is publicly held and subject to the strictures of the Sarbanes-Oxley Act (SOX), you may have to rethink that position. While the Act does not specifically address T&E and what is allowable, many experts believe that a loose T&E policy could be a sign of poor internal controls (Section 404 of the Act) and get you dinged on your SOX audit.

Thus, a growing number of companies, whether they are publicly traded or not, are tightening up their T&E policies, documenting everything and putting an end to questionable practices. They are also updating their policies on a regular basis, at least once a year, and making sure that all their employees have access to the policy.

ACCESS TO THE POLICY

The T&E policy should not contain any company secrets. It should be available to all employees who travel and those who make travel arrangements or fill out expense reports for their superiors. (We're not even going to pretend that we believe all executives fill out their own reports.) Rather than trying to determine who needs to see the policy and who doesn't, many companies now post the policy on their intranet site. The policy does not have to be printed. Given this flexibility, the policy is available to anyone at any time who needs to see the information.

Updates can be published immediately, as updating a web site is a simple task. This means there is no delay in getting information to all employees on a timely basis. It also removes another excuse for not updating the policy.

A TWO-MINUTE ASSESSMENT OF YOUR T&E PROCESS

It's really easy to go wrong when it comes to a corporate T&E policy. Just ask Thomas Coughlin, who resigned in March 2006 as Wal-Mart's vice chairman. The company has accused him of taking as much as $500,000 from unauthorized gift card transactions and fraudulent expense reports. So, how does a company with a balance sheet as strong as Wal-Mart's end up in such a mess? Without access to inside Wal-Mart information and policies, we don't know. We do know, however, how to identify gaps in corporate T&E policies. Take the quiz in Exhibit 8.1 to determine if your organization is laying any T&E landmines.

1. Does your company have a formal written T&E policy, approved by management? _____ Yes _____ No

   Potential Issue: Without a formal written policy it is impossible to mandate policy and track individual compliance. You'll also run afoul of all Sarbanes-Oxley internal control requirements.

2. Has your company's T&E policy been updated within the last 12 months? _____ Yes _____ No

   Potential Issue: All policies as well as written manuals should be updated and reviewed at least annually, if not more frequently. At a minimum, changes in per diems as well as the reimbursement rate for mileage should be updated to reflect market conditions.

3. Is everyone in the company—including the most senior officers—required to comply with the T&E policy? _____ Yes _____ No

   Potential Issue: Besides the fairness issue, the ability to monitor compliance goes right out the window if certain people are excluded. This should not be confused with differing policies for different groups of employees. For example, in some firms officers may fly first class while non-officer employees get coach seats.

4. Do you spot check T&E expense reimbursement requests instead of checking each report? _____ Yes _____ No

   Potential Issue: Verifying T&E reports is a time-consuming task that adds little value. Not checking at all is an unattractive option, too, as travelers might get a little loose with their reporting if they thought no one was watching.

5. Does your organization offer cash advances? _____ Yes _____ No

   Potential Issue: While providing cash advances to employees might seem like a fair thing to do, it usually backfires on the employer. With no money out of their pockets, many employees do not feel it necessary to file their T&E reports. However, if they need that reimbursement to pay the credit card bill, most will feel a certain urgency when it comes to filing their reports.

Exhibit 8.1   The T&E Policy Quiz: Do You Have A Problem

In the exhibit, with the exception of number 5, the correct answer to all the questions is yes. While $500,000 is just a drop in the bucket to Wal-Mart, the negative publicity associated with this alleged fraud is far more damaging. At a minimum, your T&E policy should incorporate the concepts discussed here. The days of being able to look the other way when someone violated T&E policy are fast coming to an end. Sarbanes-Oxley, corporate cost-cutting initiatives, and an overriding desire to avoid negative press are forcing companies everywhere to implement the same types of stringent controls in their T&E programs as they do in other parts of their businesses.

T&E POLICY: GOOD NEWS AND BAD

Accounts Payable Now & Tomorrow polled its readers to find out about the existence of T&E policies in the corporate world. While most executives know it is a very good idea—especially after Sarbanes-Oxley—to have a written T&E policy, we weren't sure everyone was on the same page. So we were pleased to find that 94.44% of the respondents have such a policy. That's where the good news ends, though.

While the majority is on the right track, some haven't even arrived at the station. When asked about policy updates, the responses were:

- Whenever there's a change   53.42%
- Annually   17.81%
- Can't remember the last time it was updated   6.85%
- Other   21.92%

What does *other* mean? When asked for an explanation, here's a sampling of what they had to say:

- Every two years.
- Two years ago.

- It was just implemented.
- Every three to five years.
- As needed.
- This policy is the only one ever done.
- When someone notices employees are going overboard.
- It used to be never, but as of this year it will be at least twice a year.
- The last change was in 2002 (four years ago).
- Whenever board of directors or management wants.
- Quarterly review.
- Annually plus whenever there's a change.
- We're working on it now.

We suspect that the "we're working on it now" response (given by all too many respondents) is reflective of the fundamental change in the T&E philosophy that is going on in parts of the corporate world. In another survey, readers of the same publication were asked about the effects of SOX on various functions. Although only 30% of the respondents worked at public companies, 57% indicated they were changing their T&E processes.

ADMINISTERING THE POLICY

If you've spent any time in Accounts Payable, you know that in some organizations there are two sets of rules: one for "everyone" and one for "special" employees. This is particularly true when it comes to T&E. So we asked those surveyed if all employees are held to the T&E policy across the board. Not surprisingly, a significant group reports their firm does not administer the policy uniformly. While 84.72% said their organizations held everyone to the policy, another 15.28% said their organizations did not.

One respondent, who wisely decided to remain anonymous, noted that at their company everyone but the president was held to the policy.

T&E POLICY BEST PRACTICES

It goes without saying that every organization should have a written T&E policy. It should be given to every employee who either travels or handles any T&E matters, including filling out reimbursement requests for superiors. Ideally, the policy (and all updates) should be in the hands of any travelers *before* they travel.

The policy should be updated every time there is a change and reviewed at least once a year. More frequently is fine; less frequently can lead to trouble.

The policy should be posted for everyone to see. There should be no secrets, so there is no reason to limit access. Posting on the company intranet site eliminates all sorts of problems and the no-one-told-me-that excuse.

It also goes without saying that the policy should be administered uniformly. Managers should not be allowed to okay policy violations. Not only is that not fair to other employees, it could get you into trouble in your SOX audit and, in extreme situations, with the IRS. The latter could occur if an ineligible payment was made.

POLICY SYNOPSIS

The T&E policy should spell out the guidelines for company employees when it comes to T&E. It details some or all of the following:

- What is allowable
- What is not allowable

- How documentation should be submitted
- What approvals are necessary
- Timing of reporting
- Whether cash advances are permitted and, if so, under what circumstances
- Whether corporate T&E cards must be used
- Reimbursement policy
- What hotel chains are preferred or required
- What airlines are preferred or required
- What car rental agencies are recommended or required
- Whether employees must stay over on a Saturday night if a lower fare can be obtained
- How unused tickets are to be handled

The company's T&E policy should be formal, written, and distributed to all employees for easy reference. It should be updated periodically, no less frequently than once every two years. Ideally, the update should take place every year. Changes should be reflected in the policy, which is often printed and distributed in a binder.

Printing costs can be reduced almost entirely by publishing the T&E policy on the corporate intranet site. In this way, updates can be communicated quickly.

Whenever there is a major change to the T&E policy, a memo should go out from a senior executive explaining the change. The memo, which can be paper based or sent in an e-mail, should be sent to all employees.

For a T&E policy to be effective, it has to be enforced across the board. This means that managers should not be allowed to override the policy where they think it does not apply to their staff. Obviously, for the policy to be effective it needs to be adhered to by executives at all levels.

Policy enforcement should not fall on the shoulders of the Accounts Payable department. That really is not fair. Companies using an automated system can have a policy-compliance feature built in. In these systems, reports that are in violation of the company policy are flagged for further investigation. The Accounts Payable department can then return these reports to the approver's supervisor for further review.

Some of the more advanced automated systems take policy compliance one step further. They refuse to allow the submission of reports in violation of the policy. This is a bit extreme, as there will be infrequent occasions when an expense outside the policy is justified.

New employees should be given a copy of the T&E policy as part of their welcome packet.

Ideally, there should be a focal point for questions relating to the T&E policy.

Frequent T&E policy violators should be noted and their reports checked thoroughly each time one is submitted. (See the Spot Checking section in Chapter 4.)

Senior management must support the policy in a very public way. Some companies do this effectively by having either the chief executive officer or the chief financial officer sign the cover memo that goes out with the policy. Others do it by having one of these senior officials sign a memo about T&E policy compliance that is put in the front of the T&E policy manual.

CREATING YOUR OWN T&E POLICY

If you do not currently have a written T&E policy, you'll need to create one. Similarly, if the one you have is more than a few years old, you might consider starting from scratch. It's not as hard as it might appear. Chapter 9 has a sample policy that covers most, if not all, the issues you might want to address in your policy. There are 26 sections.

Each of the sections contains one or more suggested policies. You can start by using that as a guideline, selecting the wording that most closely describes your policy, and making adjustments to reflect your actual policy where necessary.

Each organization may have special, unique issues that it wishes to address in its policy. Simply add these to the policy to make it your own.

KEEPING THE POLICY CURRENT

Getting the appropriate people to agree on the policy and getting it written the first time is probably the hardest task you'll have. But, once it's written, it's not over. The policy should be updated no less frequently than once a year. Otherwise, a few years will pass and the policy will be completely obsolete.

ENFORCING THE POLICY

This is a delicate issue. In theory, when an expense account report and reimbursement request are sent down to Accounts Payable approved by the appropriate manager, Accounts Payable should merely pay the reimbursement. Ironically, in many organizations, policy compliance falls on the shoulders of the Accounts Payable group although they don't have any real authority to enforce it.

The reality is that few managers actually check the T&E reports submitted by their subordinates. They merely approve whatever is put in front of them. The reasons for this are numerous and largely irrelevant to this discussion. The bottom line is that most expense reports are not checked or verified by the person who puts his or her signature on the approval line.

The policy should contain statements about managerial responsibility and a decision should be made internally about whether Accounts Payable is expected to check for policy compliance. Most companies do want their Accounts Payable group to check for policy compliance because they recognize that their managers are not doing it. If you make that decision, make sure that you back the managers who enforce the policy—because they are anything but popular when they do it.

Of course, an easy way around this issue is to use one of the nifty models on the market today that incorporate a policy-compliance feature. Many of these refuse to let employees enter an item that is outside the policy. This takes the burden off both the approving manager and the Accounts Payable staff. However, at this juncture, many companies are still relying on their Accounts Payable staff to check for policy compliance.

9

Sample T&E Policy Manual

INTRODUCTION

What follows is a proposed travel and entertainment (T&E) policy that would work in most organizations. It can be adapted to meet the requirements for most organizations. Note that some of the sections have several suggestions. Select the one that is closest to your policy and then modify it to meet your needs. You may find that you do not like any of the suggestions in a particular section. Simply write your own to meet your own requirements.

SECTION 1: POLICY APPROVAL

Who Approved the Policy: _____ [Ideally one or more very senior officers]

Last Amended Date: _____

Next Review Date: _____ [No more than 12 months after the last amended date]

83

SECTION 2: T&E POLICY STATEMENT

[The policy should start with a statement. Here are several that could work.]

- Spend the company's money as though it were your own.
- This travel and entertainment policy applies to all employees who incur expenses while engaged in company business. Only those expenses that have been incurred while on company business will be reimbursed. Company travel, entertainment, and other business expense reimbursement program meets the Internal Revenue Service (IRS) definition of reimbursable expense. *Expenses that conform to this policy are not reported as taxable income to the individual.* Certain expenditures that do not conform to this policy will not be considered reimbursable under policy. Items of a personal nature incurred while traveling shall be carefully segregated from company expenses and are not reimbursable. All travel, entertainment, and other business-related expenses must be made within the ethical and legal limits as defined by industry, state, and federal regulations.
- It is corporate policy to reimburse employees for all necessary travel and other expenses incurred while engaged in conducting corporate business. In applying this policy, it is intended that the accommodations and services required shall be of a standard of quality that will adequately meet the needs of the employees from the standpoint of both comfort and appropriateness for the effective conduct of business.

  Individuals incurring T&E expenses on behalf of the company must exercise prudence and judgment. Expenses should be within reasonable limits and commensurate with the nature of the business assignment and the capacity in which the individual represents the corporation. Expenses that do not help achieve company objectives, or are not reasonable under the circumstances, or are of a personal nature will not be reimbursed. [This wording courtesy of DataServ's Kelly Tripp.]

[Also may include corporate mission statement.]
[Also may include corporate vision.]

SECTION 3: POLICY PURPOSE

The purpose of this policy is to provide broad guidelines for official business travel and entertainment, in accordance with applicable regulations and sound business practices.

SECTION 4: EXCEPTIONS TO THE POLICY

Division Vice Presidents or their designees have sole authority to approve exceptions to provisions of this policy. Approved exceptions must be in writing and submitted when business expenses are sent to the Accounts Payable Department. Approved exceptions must be explicitly justified as beneficial to both the company and the individual and generally require the recommendation of the individual's supervisor.

SECTION 5: EMPLOYEE RESPONSIBILITIES RELATED TO T&E

The following is the responsibility of every traveling employee:

- Verify that all expenses being paid or reimbursed are valid and conform to the provisions established in this policy, and understand that requests lacking required documentation will not be reimbursed.

- Ensure that expenses submitted for reimbursement have not been previously paid through a business expense report, by cash advance, or by an outside organization.
- An individual shall not approve his/her own expenses. In addition, approvals may not be granted by any subordinate within the direct reporting structure of the individual requesting the expenditure or reimbursement.
- Submit all forms related to his/her travel within 30 days of completion of travel or business event. The employee incurring expenses may delegate responsibility for preparation of the appropriate forms but will always retain accountability for ensuring all travel, entertainment, or business expenses are in accordance with this policy and in compliance with company requirements.
- If using a company procurement card, submit transaction detail with notes on the travel and entertainment report. If using personal credit card or for "out of pocket" expenses, submit a copy of the credit card bill along with the receipts.

SECTION 6: PREFERRED METHOD OF PAYMENT

The Company Procurement Card is the preferred method of payment for goods and services as well as corporate travel. Expenses charged to the Company Procurement Card must be settled/submitted within fifteen (15) days following the end of the cardholder's billing cycle in which the charges appear. For purchases on the procurement card, both the employee and supervisor are still responsible for complying with this policy, such that only appropriate expenses are paid from company funds.

SECTION 7: SUPERVISOR RESPONSIBILITIES RELATED TO T&E

Individuals authorized to approve travel, entertainment, or business expenditures of other employees will administer this policy. Expenses that appear to be excessive or unusual in relation to the nature of the business travel shall be investigated prior to approval. Explanation of any such expenditure must be included on business expense reporting before submission to Accounts Payable.

Transactions and forms related to travel, entertainment, or business expenses must be approved by next-level supervisor. The authorized approver is responsible for verifying the purpose of the expense is valid and directly related to official company business. Reimbursement reports submitted for approval should be reviewed and approved within five (5) business days. Approved expense reports should be forwarded by the approver to Accounts Payable. The employee should be informed that his or her report has been sent to Accounts Payable.

SECTION 8: ACCOUNTS PAYABLE RESPONSIBILITIES RELATED TO T&E

Accounts Payable is responsible for reviewing all approved T&E expense reports and investigating all policy noncompliance. All forms related to travel, entertainment, or business expense must be sent to the Accounts Payable Department within thirty (30) days of end of the trip. Accounts Payable must verify that expenses are reasonable and meet the following criteria:

- Information contained on detail matches notes by T&E report or report of business expense and the accompanying support documentation is complete and in accordance with the policy.

- Expenses conform to any requirements imposed by the Internal Revenue Service (IRS).
- Expenses are charged to proper accounts.
- Expenses have been reviewed/approved by next-level supervisor.

SECTION 9: RECEIPTS

IRS regulations require receipts for any expenditure in excess of $75.

[Many organizations lower this amount. Some alternatives that you can choose from are:

- Require receipts for any expenditure.
- Require receipts for all expenditures in excess of $10.
- Require receipts for all expenditures in excess of $25.
- Require receipts for all expenditures in excess of $75. Most companies rely on the $25.]

Additionally, all hotel folios with detail should be submitted. [The reason for this is the IRS does not allow 100% deductibility for certain expenses such as meals.]

SECTION 10: WHO PAYS WHEN MORE THAN ONE EMPLOYEE IS INVOLVED

- When two or more employees travel together on company business and expense and jointly incur expenses, except in unusual circumstances, each shall pay and separately record his/her own expenses.
- When two or more employees are involved in an event where only one bill is presented, the highest-ranking individual shall pay the bill and request reimbursement. In no event shall an executive approve a reimbursement expense

if he or she was a participant in a reimbursement covered by that request.

SECTION 11: WHAT'S COVERED

The following types of expenses, if reasonable and necessary, for company business purposes, and if properly documented, are examples of expenses that may be payable or reimbursable as defined in this Policy:

- *Air and rail travel.* This may also include change or cancellation penalties imposed by the airlines if due to unavoidable circumstances (supporting documentation must be supplied with the T&E form).
- *Alcoholic beverages* purchased in conjunction with official company business entertainment are allowable (if they do not appear on the not-covered list).
- *Car rental, gasoline, and oil* for rental vehicles.
- *Ground transportation,* including taxi and public transportation fares, mileage for personal vehicles, parking fees, and tolls.
- *Laundry/dry cleaning* during trips longer than five (5) calendar days.
- *Lodging.*
- *Meals and entertainment* while on official company business.
- *Miscellaneous* (room service, luggage storage, and valet).
- *Registration and fees* for attendance at approved conferences and seminars (to prepay, use an online requisition or the procurement card as appropriate).
- *Taxes* associated with transportation, lodging, and meals.
- *Tips associated with lodging, meals, and transportation* if customary.

- *Travel to and from an airport* calculated at the rate per mile established by the IRS. If a second party drives the traveler to an airport and picks him or her up after the trip, the traveler may be reimbursed for two roundtrips (but not more than the cost of other available means of transport).

SECTION 12: WHAT'S NOT COVERED

[To avoid problems it is a good idea to spell out what is not covered. Select those items that you wish to exclude and add any that are not included. It is better to be safe than end up in a debate with an employee who is not exercising good judgment.]

The following expenses will *not* be reimbursed by the company:

- Personal grooming services, such as barbers, hairdressers, and shoe shines
- Car rental insurance purchased for domestic travel
- Childcare
- Membership to private clubs
- Airport airline clubs
- Fees for frequent-flyer programs and other similar awards for hotel and car rentals
- Fitness and recreational fees, including massages and saunas
- In-room movies
- Insurance costs, such as life insurance, flight insurance, personal automobile insurance, and baggage insurance
- Lost baggage
- Loss or theft of cash advance funds, airline tickets, personal funds or property
- "No-show" charges for hotel and car service

- Parking tickets or traffic violations
- Personal automobile repairs
- Personal credit card annual or late fees
- Personal telephone charges in excess of reasonable calls home, generally one per day
- Pet care
- Upgrades (air, hotel, car, etc.)
- Spouse or guest travel
- Liquor
- Limousine service, unless no other more cost-effective mode of transportation exists

SECTION 13: CASH ADVANCES

[Depending on your corporate policy, pick one of the following:]

- *The no cash advance policy.* Except in extreme circumstances, the company does not offer cash advances. If one is needed, it should be documented and approved by a vice president at least five (5) days before the travel is to begin.
- *If cash advances are allowed.* All travelers are eligible for advances of $100 per day up to a maximum of $500 per week for reasonable out-of-pocket travel expenses. The preferred method of obtaining travel advances is via an ATM withdrawal using the traveler's company-issued procurement card. ATM advances should not be taken more than three days before the expected travel or expense. Cash advances at ATMs overseas are dispensed in local currency at an advantageous exchange rate.

  Travelers may check with the procurement card program office to determine the availability of ATMs in their destination country.

Alternatively, the company's travel advance policy allows travelers to request advances in the form of a direct deposit (depending on their payroll setup) or by a check issued by Accounts Payable within two (2) weeks of travel dates. Allow at least five (5) business days for check preparation.

Travel advances must be accounted for on a T&E form within thirty (30) days after return. Travel advances secured via the procurement card must be accounted for within fifteen (15) days following the end of the billing cycle in which they appear on a cardholder's monthly statement. Any excess advances must be repaid within thirty (30) days of the time of accounting for the advance. Unaccounted travel advances have personal income tax consequences for the traveler.

SECTION 14: AIRLINE SERVICE

[If there is a preferred carrier, list it in the policy.]

Additional airline requirements:

- All domestic and international air travel must be in coach or equivalent class.
- Employees are expected to use the lowest airfare available. Exceptions may be allowed if written approval is secured in advance. With prior approval, the following exceptions may be allowed if the lowest-priced airfare would:
  - Require travel during unreasonable hours
  - Excessively prolong travel
  - Greatly increase the duration of the flight
  - Result in increased costs that would offset transportation savings

○   Be inadequate for the medical needs or physical conditions/disabilities of the traveler

○   Require overnight flights

Documentation of this approval must accompany the related business expense reporting. Divisional vice president will approve exceptions.

Business class is acceptable when it does *not* cost more than the lowest available coach class.

[Note: You may allow first-class travel for excessively long flights. Spell out what excessively long is; typically over eight hours.]

SECTION 15: DENIED BOARDING COMPENSATION

Airlines occasionally offer free tickets or cash allowances to compensate travelers for delays and inconveniences due to overbooking, flight cancellations, changes of equipment, and so on. Travelers may volunteer for denied boarding compensation only if the delay in their trip will not result in any interruption of business or any additional costs. In these cases, the employee is free to keep the compensation.

SECTION 16: UNUSED/VOIDED TICKET

Unused transportation tickets or flight coupons must never be discarded or destroyed as these documents may have a cash value. To expedite refunds, unused or partially used tickets must be returned immediately to the local agency office that issued the ticket. It is the employee's responsibility to understand the refund policies for selected transportation carrier.

If an employee is traveling on an e-ticket, please notify the travel office immediately.

SECTION 17: RENTAL CARS

The company will reimburse travelers for the cost of renting a mid-size, intermediate, or compact car and for automobile-related expenses. The company has discounted rates available at ABC Car Rental Agency. Employees must use that agency if one is available. Mileage is not reimbursable for rental vehicle, although the cost of gasoline may be reimbursed. Additional guidelines include:

- Travelers should rent a car to their destination when driving is more cost-effective than other means of transportation.
- When picking up a rental car, travelers should check with the rental car agent for any promotional rates, last-minute specials, or free upgrades.
- The physical condition of the rental vehicle should be inspected prior to leaving the rental lot. Any damage found should be reported to the car rental agency before the vehicle is accepted. Damage should be documented on the car rental agreement to avoid possible dispute over damages for which the company is not responsible.
- When renting vehicles for company business, it is not necessary to purchase any auto insurance offered by rental agencies.
- Original rental agreement and any associated gasoline receipts must be submitted with business expense reporting.
- Employees will not be reimbursed for traffic citations they receive while on company business.
- Travelers are responsible for canceling rental car reservations if travel plans change.

SECTION 18: GROUND TRANSPORTATION

Taxi, bus, subway, or shuttle fares will be reimbursed at actual cost. Receipts should include dates, destination, and amounts. Employees traveling to the same location should share ground transportation to and from the airport whenever possible.

Local car service may be used if it is the most economical form of transportation.

Limousines or car services should be used *only* when valid business reasons preclude the use of more economical modes of transportation.

SECTION 19: USE OF PERSONAL AUTOMOBILE

A privately owned vehicle may be used for business travel provided the vehicle is insured by the private owner and the individual using such a vehicle has a valid operator's license. It is expressly understood that while using a privately owned vehicle, the operator assumes all responsibility for accidents to the extent of the operator's insurance coverage.

The company will pay a standard rate per mile for official travel by private automobile based on the actual driving distance by the most direct route. Under normal circumstances, mileage is computed from the traveler's normal place of business to the destination and return to the traveler's normal place of business.

Currently, reimbursement is at the rate of 44.5 cents per mile. This rate will adjust as the federal government adjusts its rate, typically effective January 1 each year.

Employees may not request reimbursement for gas. This is covered by the 44.5 cents. However, they may request reimbursement for all tolls paid in the course of company business.

SECTION 20: PREFERRED HOTELS

The company has contracts with ABC Hotels and DEF Hotels. Please stay in these hotels whenever your travel permits. Make sure when you register that you identify yourself as an employee of our company.

The company will reimburse travelers for the single-occupancy cost of a standard room. Travelers should always select a hotel that is the most economical for their business trips, if it is not one of the preferred hotels.

When traveling to a conference, it is appropriate to stay at the hotel hosting the conference, assuming that the daily rate is not unreasonably expensive relative to other alternatives.

SECTION 21: LODGING RECEIPTS

All lodging receipts are required. Meals and incidentals on lodging receipts must be itemized separately. A lodging receipt must include all of the following information:

- Name and location of the lodging establishment
- Dates of stay
- Itemized charges for lodging, meals, telephone calls, and so on

Employees are encouraged to use their own cell phones for all calls and discouraged, except in cases of emergency, from using phones in their hotel rooms.

Receipts for lodging are always required. All other non-meal expenses require dated, original receipts. Receipts must be submitted when reporting business expenses.

SECTION 22: MEALS AND INCIDENTALS: FOR EMPLOYEE ONLY

The company will reimburse a traveler for allowable meal and incidental expenses incurred during company-related travel.

[You can reimburse either on a per diem basis or actual expense basis. Pick one of the following depending on your policy:]

- *Per diem.* Per diem allowance includes meals and tips for foodservice handlers at restaurants. Meals must be itemized separately on lodging receipts. Receipts and detailed documentation are not required when requesting reimbursement of meals using the per diem option. [Some firms will require the receipts. If you require receipts, the policy should clearly indicate at what level receipts are expected.]

  The allowable per diem depends on the location of the travel. [Use the table in Appendix A to determine your per diem. Most companies base their allowable per diems on the rates set by the federal government for its workers. These are set each year on or about October 1. Appendix A has the rates set on October 1, 2006. You can find updated rates on www.gsa.gov.]

- *Actual cost.* The company will reimburse travelers for three (3) meals a day. On the days of travel to or from the destination, the individual's departure and return times should determine whether a meal occurred during the period of travel.

  Receipts for any meal in excess of $25 are required.

  Total daily meals in excess of $50 require supporting receipts.

SECTION 23: EXPENSES FOR MEALS FOR OTHERS

Travelers sometimes pay for meals for others. These expenses are reimbursable when the name(s) of the meal attendees are listed and the business purpose of the meal is justified. A traveler may not submit a per diem request for a meal if his or her meal was included in a group bill paid for by someone else.

Restaurant receipts must include all of the following information:

- Name and location of the restaurant
- Number of people served
- Date and amount of expense

Gratuities should be shown on the credit card receipt.

The restaurant chosen for the entertainment should be reasonable for the location and purpose of the meal. Extravagant expenditures will be denied.

SECTION 24: TRAVEL EXPENSES OF
SPOUSE/PERSONAL GUEST

The expenses of a spouse, family member, or guest accompanying the business traveler are not reimbursable. The company will not reimburse spouse/personal guest travel expenses when a spouse/personal guest attends a meeting or conference and has no significant role or performs only incidental duties. Such attendance does not constitute a valid business purpose.

Spouse/personal guest expenses should not be charged directly to the company and then later reimbursed by the individual. These are considered personal expenses.

When a spouse/personal guest attends a function and has a significant role in the proceedings or is involved in fundraising activities, this constitutes a valid business purpose. Prior to travel for fundraising purposes, all reimbursed spousal/personal guest travel must be approved by the appropriate vice president. This approval must be obtained in writing prior to the event.

In these rare cases the company will reimburse the business traveler for the spouse's/personal guest's nonpersonal expenses directly resulting from travel on company business. The business purpose for the spouse/personal guest expenses must be stated when reporting business expenses.

Note: Other expenses for spouses/personal guests of travelers, if reimbursed as an approved exception, are taxable and included on the employee's payroll records as taxable income.

SECTION 25: ENTERTAINMENT

On occasion, it is appropriate to provide a meal or reasonably priced entertainment for business contacts. These events must be related to company business and the job responsibilities of the company representative.

To qualify as entertainment under IRS guidelines, entertainment expenses must be "directly related to" or "associated with" business. Substantial business discussion must take place immediately before, during, or after the entertainment.

All entertainment expenses, including local entertaining and entertaining while traveling, must be itemized when reporting business expenses.

The following entertainment expenses are reimbursable:

- Sporting event tickets
- Concert and theater tickets
- Transportation to/from the event
- Meals and beverages consumed at the event

If there is any question as to whether an expense is appropriate, inquire before the event rather than after.

The following documentation is required by the IRS when documenting business and expense reports:

- Date(s) entertainment occurred
- Who was entertained? (Persons or group; names, titles, business relationships)
- What was the event?
- Where was the event?
- Why? (Business purpose/reason for entertaining)

SECTION 26: NON-TRAVEL BUSINESS EXPENSE REIMBURSEMENT

Reimbursable expenses include:

- Retail purchases of supplies, books, and other low-cost items required for business purposes.
- Expenses associated with business meetings as long as they are reasonable and directly associated with company business.
- Expenses incurred by company employees, including employees who incur expenses on behalf of another or nonemployees. These may be reimbursed from company funds if the expenditures have a direct connection with company functions and business.
- Reasonable expenses for improvement of working conditions, employer–employee relations, and employee performance recognition. Examples of items in this section include employee morale activities such as a holiday party, summer picnic, employment anniversary celebration, or retirement party. It is important to identify on the expense report the purpose of employer–employee relations expenditures and the names of individuals or groups involved.

- Non-cash gifts under $75. In some cases, the company may give inexpensive, non-cash gifts, such as gift certificates, company apparel, or other tokens of appreciation to employees, students, and guests. Individuals can purchase these gifts with personal funds and request reimbursement with department approval.

SECTION 27: WHOM TO CALL WITH QUESTIONS

- Controller
- Accounts Payable
- Purchasing
- Procurement card staff
- Travel staff

SECTION 28: OTHER

[Add whatever you feel is necessary to meet your own requirements.]

10

SOLUTIONS TO DAY-TO-DAY T&E OPERATIONAL PROBLEMS

INTRODUCTION

Travel and entertainment (T&E) brings out the worst of the petty problems that plague the corporate world. Since the funds involved are often personal, the issues take on a whole new dimension. An employee who is blasé about a million-dollar accounting issue may turn into just the opposite when it comes to a $1,200 T&E reimbursement that is needed to pay a personal credit card bill in the next few days. This chapter looks at the more common problems that occur in the T&E world and offers solutions. While nothing is perfect, hopefully you will find some guidance in the suggestions that follow, usually based on some real-life successes.

┌─── In the Real World: Confessions of a T&E Laggard ───┐

If the road to hell is paved with good intentions, I'd certainly have created a finely lined path with my intentions when it came to my T&E reimbursement reports. I'd complete my reimbursement reports every six to nine months spending an ugly day doing so. When I'd finish and turn them in I'd promise myself, "Never again." I'd do them once a month as we were supposed to.

And, let me tell you, not only are they easier to complete if you do them on a timely basis but the employee loses less money. I can't tell you how often I'd forget to fill in the cab fare on those silly little slips they give you, and then not having a clue what the cab fare had been, I did not request reimbursement. Needless to say, small-dollar out-of-pocket expenditures were rarely reported, as six months after the fact I'd completely forgotten about them.

So why didn't I turn them in as I was supposed to? The answer is quite simple. I was tardy because they let me be. Like most other employees I was overworked and there was always something more important that had to be done. I quickly learned that if I ignored the reminders that the Accounts Payable manager sent, nothing happened. Since the company paid the credit card bill and I was a pro at charging most of my expenses, I did not have a huge financial incentive to complete my reports.

The moral of this story is that for some employees there have to be consequences for not turning in their reports on time; otherwise they won't—even honorable employees who have the best of intentions.

UNEVEN POLICY ENFORCEMENT

As noted in Chapter 9, most companies do apply their policy uniformly to everyone. However, a small but significant group—approximately 15%—does not. This can lead to poor morale and also set the stage for employees to try and pad their expense reports. After all, the rationale goes, if Joe in purchasing can order $100 bottles of wine, why shouldn't the low-level accounting manager get an extra $25 by submitting phony taxi receipts?

Since corporate culture is something that starts at the top, the very best way to have complete enforcement of the policy is for the president and other top-ranking executives conform to the policy and require that their lieutenants do the same. If this situation is present, policy-compliance issues drop drastically.

Begin by including a statement in the T&E policy that makes it clear that everyone is expected to conform to the policy. This combined with compliance at the top is a very easy way to set the tone.

If you use one of the automated T&E systems that include a policy-compliance module, the battle is over. Most of these systems will not allow an employee to enter something that is out of compliance. Of course, the systems are not foolproof. Crafty employees will find ways to get around the compliance, entering amounts as something that they are not. Still, the automated checking takes a lot of the burden off Accounts Payable.

If that option is not available, may companies empower their Accounts Payable staff to reject requests that are submitted in violation of the policy. This is where there needs to be a policy regarding what is expected of Accounts Payable. Recognizing that many managers will approve virtually anything submitted by their employees, some companies give them the ability to reject a claim. Others put the onus on the manager and simply expect the Accounts Payable staff to pay whatever comes through approved. The controller or chief financial officer (CFO) should make a decision on this issue and then back the Accounts Payable staff if the decision is to empower Accounts Payable to reject the claim. Alas, although the decision is often made to let Accounts Payable reject an unsuitable reimbursement, when push comes to shove, management backs off and allows the payment. This is not a good situation and causes morale to plummet in Accounts Payable.

There is another way around this ugly issue that tends to solve the problem and not make anyone too unhappy. Let's face it, no matter how hard you try and write a fair and equitable policy, there are always going to be times when it is appropriate for the policy to be overridden. But, who should make that decision?

Many companies have gotten around this problem by requiring an authorization from a supervisor one level above the normal approver for all T&E policy exceptions. Faced with the requirement of having to explain why they need to be reimbursed outside the company policy to their boss's boss, many employees will forgo the reimbursement. In fact, they may not make the expenditure in the first place. This policy provides flexibility where needed and will generally result in very few exceptions being requested. Require that this authorization be done in writing.

There is another variation of this approach that works, but it is not quite so nice. Make it an accepted procedure that when a T&E report is submitted with an approval for an expense outside the company policy, Accounts Payable automatically sends it to the approver's superior with a note asking whether it should be paid. This puts both the approver and the submitter in the hot seat. Once it becomes known that this is the process (and you might include wording about this in your policy), the number of policy violations will decline. In fact, if there is one highly publicized incident, the issue of policy compliance could become a nonevent. Whether this is appropriate for your organization is a question of corporate culture and management's view on this issue. If yours is favorable, you might want to try this approach.

TOUGH TACTICS TO GET T&E REPORTS SUBMITTED ON TIME!

Anyone involved in T&E processing for more than a few months becomes painfully aware that it is difficult to get certain employees to submit their T&E reimbursement forms on a timely basis. Let's face it, filling out a T&E report and attaching all those annoying receipts is not a whole lot of fun. The problem is exacerbated in those organizations where the company pays the credit card bill. There, employees have little incentive to get their reports turned in on time. Or do they? We asked Accounts Payable professionals about this in a recent survey. Here are some tactics they use with great success:

- Submit a report each month to the president of the company. It contains the employees' names and receipt dates.
- Have an e-mail go out under the president's name (or that of some other high-level executive) asking for the late reports. Most people only have to get this note once.
- Inform senior managers and supervisors of late or missing reports.
- Do not provide any reimbursements to employees who have outstanding expense reports.
- Deactivate the credit cards until required documentation is submitted.
- Require that the employee pay all late credit card charges. Actually, the organization that uses this approach gives the employees one pass, paying the charges the first time.
- Credit card payment is not made until T&E report is received.
- Send correspondence to the employee with escalations to increasing levels of management if the employee does not resolve the matter.

- Do not provide cash advances. If the company insists on offering them to traveling employees, restrict this privilege to those who are not late with their reports.
- If an employee receives an advance and does not submit a report within 30 days, the employee's manager is called in to explain to the division director.

Are you cringing reading this? Yes, the tactics described are harsh. But getting T&E reports submitted on time is important and sometimes it takes a tough approach to get the matter resolved.

LESS HARSH METHODS OF GETTING THE LAGGARDS TO TURN IN REPORTS ON TIME

Getting reports turned in on time is an issue for certain Accounts Payable departments. You can begin by spelling out the corporate expectations in the policy. This sets the stage and can make the timing a policy-compliance issue. If your organization is not willing to take the steps described in the previous section—and many aren't—try some of these less draconian tactics:

- Send out a reminder e-mail to everyone at your company who travels several days before your check run cutoff, reminding all travelers of your reimbursement deadlines.
- Give every traveler one Get-Out-of-Jail-Free card. This will enable them to get a last-minute reimbursement, if they have the necessary documentation approved. While this will guarantee a certain number of Rush checks, it serves notice that each traveler will be accommodated only once. This is useful if you are at a company that will require you to issue the Rush check. If you want to have a very strict policy of never reimbursing people outside the normal check production cycle, do not use this technique.

- Provide each new employee with your policy and procedures regarding T&E reimbursement. Try and narrow it down to a one-page cheat sheet. Otherwise, they are unlikely to read it.
- Give your one-page cheat sheet to any employee who requests a last-minute reimbursement along with their check.
- Refuse to give cash advances to the traveling employee until the prior advance has been accounted for (assuming you give cash advances in the first place).

Every problem presents an opportunity and don't overlook this one: If you are trying to convert everyone to automated clearinghouse (ACH) reimbursements, limit your last-minute accommodations to payment via the ACH. If you can get away with it, insist that the employee continue to be reimbursed that way.

THE RUSH CHECK ISSUE: IS IT THE EMPLOYEE OR THE SUPERVISOR?

In organizations where employees are expected to use their own credit card, there can be another problem. Most employees need their reimbursement to pay the upcoming credit card bill. Now, if you think that this impending financial obligation is enough to keep all employees turning in their T&E reports on time, you would be only 95% accurate. There are a small number who like to live on the edge and will wait until the bill is just about due before they complete their report. Then they run it in for approval and down to Accounts Payable expecting the staff to drop everything and cut them a check.

In case you haven't guessed, Accounts Payable has heard the "my-credit-card-bill-is-due tomorrow" story so many times that they are not likely to be swayed by it. This creates a bit of animosity between Accounts Payable and the employee with the looming bill. The issue gets even thornier when the employee did turn the report in on time but the supervisor neglected to review and approve it.

From both an efficiency standpoint as well as an internal controls point, it is not a good idea for Accounts Payable to stop everything and issue a reimbursement check simply because an employee needs it. While it may be understandable in the case where the boss has not taken the time to review it, it is still poor practice to issue the check. If the employee is at fault, employ the suggestions in the prior section about those who are tardy in submitting their reports, and if it is the supervisor, try some of the tactics suggested in the next section.

Having said all this, there needs to be a modicum of human compassion when it comes to this issue. It is suggested that every employee be given one chance. Reimburse them on a Rush basis once using the ACH, not a check, with a warning that they just used up their one-time exemption. Alternatively, as with any other Rush check, require approval from a senior manager or the supervisor of the person requesting the Rush. Of course, if the manager is the problem, requiring his signature for the Rush payment is not really a workable solution.

APPROVALS: DEALING WITH THE
FOOT-DRAGGING MANAGER

Most of the time, when a manager does not approve his or her employees' T&E expense reports, it is simply because the manager has too many other things to do. Occasionally it is something else. If your Accounts Payable staff is not careful, they can find themselves drawn into an ongoing battle between a boss and a subordinate. This can happen when the boss and the subordinate, for whatever reason, are not getting along. One of the ways the boss retaliates is to not approve the T&E expense report. If the employee needs the funds to pay her credit card, she is put in an awkward position. Often, in these circumstances, she will try and get Accounts Payable to act as the middleperson. This is not what you are paying the Accounts Payable staff for and it is a lose-lose situation for them.

The reason for the lack of approval is not the concern for the person handling the T&E expense process. It should not become his or her problem. There are several ways that the Accounts Payable staff can deal with this issue. Begin by ignoring whatever problems may be going on between the boss and the subordinate, if that is an issue. If you have sent out a reminder e-mail to employees about their T&E reports and several state that the reports have been submitted but their managers have not yet approved them, immediately send a memorandum e-mail to the approvers reminding them of the upcoming cutoff dates.

After a while you will get to know who are the regulars, when it comes to forgetting to approve reports. Automatically send them a reminder e-mail notice. Some professionals automatically send all approvers such a reminder each payment cycle. There is one thing you should keep in mind about these e-mails. After a while, the employees will already know what your e-mails say. If they are gently nagging ones, as these reminders tend to be, the staff won't open them.

So, make sure the information in the subject line conveys your message. The message line could say something like: June 12: Cutoff date for T&E reimbursements. While this is certainly not worthy of any literary award, it will convey the needed information to your employees and approvers. And, since they haven't opened the e-mail, the message will stand out because it will remain bolded in many systems.

If you are sending reminder e-mails to approvers, copy the employee on the message. That way the employee can put some pressure on the manager and increase the odds of your receiving the approved report within your timeframe.

Finally, if you cannot get the necessary approval, escalate it to the approver's boss. While this tactic is not likely to win many friends, it is extremely effective. Few people have to do it more than once. You can clearly state your time requirements for escalation in your T&E policy. In this way, no one can claim you blindsided them. If you want, information about potential escalations can be included in reminder e-mails.

WHERE DO I SIGN?: MANAGERS WHO APPROVE ANYTHING

At the opposite end of the spectrum, and frankly more common, are those managers who sign any expense report that is placed in front of them, often without even looking at what is on the report. If I had to hazard a guess, I'd bet that at least half of all T&E reports submitted are approved with little or no review. Thus, when it comes to policy compliance, the approving manager is usually not the first line of defense.

The very best way to get managers to review before signing is to make them just as liable as their employees for policy noncompliance. This needs to be spelled out in the company T&E policy and enforced. There are several ways to get managers' attention if the situation needs to be addressed in your organization.

The first is to have some high-level executive take all the T&E reports submitted in one week, month, or whatever is appropriate for your organization and call or e-mail all managers who have approved any report with even the tiniest of violations and ask for an explanation. Now, the executive does not have to review all the reports and find the exceptions himself or herself. Someone on staff can do that and mark them for the executive.

This is the kind of harsh action that is needed if the corporate culture has been that more or less anything goes on T&E and the company wishes to change that stance. It may be necessary if your company wishes to avoid being dinged in its Sarbanes-Oxley audit. Will it work? How would you like to be the manager who has to explain to the CFO why you approved an expense for a visit to a "gentlemen's club"?

The company can give Accounts Payable the authority to reject any report that has something in it that violates the company policy. As discussed above, require a written authorization from the person one level above the normal approver for all policy exceptions.

Another method, as discussed in the section on uneven policy enforcement, is to automatically escalate all T&E reports one level if any policy abuses are discovered.

Sometimes management does not think that this is a big issue. And, they could be right. To determine whether your managers' lack of attention to T&E detail is a problem, track the problem for one month. Have Accounts Payable keep copies of all T&E policy infractions it finds and calculate the total cost. With this dollar amount in hand, decide whether it is worth pursuing the matter with management. The relevant dollar amount will vary from organization to organization.

Finally, after a while, the professionals who process T&E reports come to know which executives will sign anything and which are rigorous in checking the details before putting their signatures on their employees' requests. Check all the reports of the employees who work for managers known for their lackadaisical approach to reviewing T&E reports—and if fraud is ever discovered, make a big deal out of it. Sometimes, unfortunately, it takes something going wrong to get people's attention. Look at the Pittsburgh Steelers' Ben Roethlisberger's refusal to wear a helmet while riding a motorcycle. Only after being involved in a serious accident did he see the light.

ONE-SIZE POLICY FOR ALL: DEALING WITH NONCOMPLIANCE ISSUES

No matter how generous your T&E policy, there will always be a few employees who think that it is not fair or that the company is expecting them to travel below their standards. The executive who requires expensive wine, the assistant vice president who insists on first-class travel, even for short distances, the manager who can't believe the company expects him to find breakfast for $10, or worse. The list is endless. Clearly some are worse than others. No one is going to suggest that spending an extra $2 for breakfast is in the same league with ordering a $100 bottle of wine for dinner with a colleague.

Policy noncompliance issues have been touched on in several of the preceding sections. To ensure maximum policy compliance (only in rare instances will you get 100% compliance), start with a statement in the formal policy that requires all employees to conform to the policy, no exceptions.

If there has been a problem or noncompliance appears to be increasing, craft a message for the president (or other high-level executive) to send to the company reminding employees of the policy and the corporate requirement that all comply. Be careful how it is worded in case some disgruntled employee decides to share your message with the press. You will want to make sure that the message cannot be interpreted as the company having financial difficulties.

Policy compliance starts at the top. So, everyone including the company president should comply with the policy. No one should be exempted. Perhaps the best example comes from the company president who submits a receipt for every last cent he includes on his expense report. One of his lieutenants jokes about the guy on the highway getting a receipt for the 25-cent toll. "That's our president," he likes to tell people.

Finally, the best way to end policy noncompliance is to simply not pay for things that fall outside the policy. This is another of those techniques that has to be applied only a few times before employees get the message.

FRAUD OR AN HONEST MISTAKE?

Several years ago I was purchasing china at a Royal Doulton store. The bill was slightly over $1,000. As I was chatting with the clerk and without paying much attention, I handed over my American Express card. Luckily I took a second look. It wasn't my personal card, but rather my corporate card. I was horrified and able to rectify the mistake before any damage was done. It was an honest mistake and one that has happened to thousands of others. How do you differentiate that error from the employee who intentionally uses the card for personal expenditures, fully intending to stick the company with the bill?

While my thousand-dollar purchase at a Royal Doulton store would have stood out like a sore thumb when my corporate bill showed up, a $200 expenditure at a restaurant would not. T&E fraud is discussed extensively in Chapter 11, so it will not be addressed in this one. Remember, fraud is most frequently committed by long-term, trusted employees, so don't let a person's tenure lull you into feeling secure on the fraud front.

If you suspect fraud, there are a few things that you can do. Start by putting the person in question on your "cowboy" list. That is the list of employees whose expense reports because of past actions are always checked completely in full detail. The employees in question generally are not informed that they are on this list.

If there is a transaction that is suspect, pull out the last few T&E reports of the employee in question. Look them over as one package. Occasionally a pattern will emerge; or worse, you'll discover that the employee is requesting reimbursement for the same expense using the same receipt on multiple reports.

While you don't want to give an employee a hard time for an honest mistake, you do want to if fraud is an issue. If something was submitted that should not have been, demand reimbursement in the strongest terms. If you are 100% certain that the expense was not legitimate, copy the appropriate high-level executive on the demand. But, be careful: If you are not correct in your assumption, and the expense turns out to be legitimate, you will not only have to apologize to the employee, but also make sure that the executive you copied is now informed that the allegation was false. Basically, I would not copy the executive until the employee had admitted to the issue.

Once the employee admitted cheating, they should go to the top of the list of those whose reports are checked in-depth each month—assuming the company chooses to continue to employ him.

UNUSED TICKETS

Today virtually all domestic travel and most international travel are done on the basis of an e-ticket. When paper tickets were issued, they served as a reminder to the traveler who had not used them that he or she needed to take care of getting reimbursed or using them at a later date. In this paperless age, that reminder is no more. And, don't think the airlines are going to remind you that you have an unused ticket out there.

Since many business travelers now purchase nonrefundable tickets, they are then faced with a ticket that can be used only against future travel and not refunded. Thus, it is necessary to keep track of these tickets. Even if the ticket can be refunded, it is necessary that someone take the necessary steps to get the refund. Travel departments should help get these refunds, if your company uses one. More likely, your travelers will handle this bit of housekeeping themselves.

One way to ensure they do something is to require that boarding passes be submitted to document travel. No boarding pass; no reimbursement.

A formal process can be put in place to handle unused tickets if this is a large enough issue at your organization. American Express says that more than 4% of e-tickets issued by corporate travel departments go unused. Fortunately, new systems have emerged to track unused e-tickets and even process refunds; however, many companies are unaware of these systems. Large companies can take advantage of this new software.

If tickets are put on a corporate card, track them against the boarding passes submitted with your travelers' T&E expense reports.

Make sure your policy regarding unused tickets is spelled out in your T&E manual. Make it clear that converting unused tickets to tickets for personal use will be considered fraud in your organization.

Finally, if you are using one of the new booking portals that provide all sorts of nifty reporting, use the unused credit reports that many of them have to track outstanding unused tickets and ensure they are used before additional funds are spent.

THE RESERVATION GAME

Here's a game that T&E fraudsters sometimes play. To make this work, reimbursement has to be on the employee's card, not the company card. As anyone who travels is painfully aware, the price of an airline ticket dances all over the place with little rhyme or reason to those outside the airline industry. The result is that two people flying on the same plane may have paid vastly different prices for those tickets. Here's what an employee looking to make a few bucks at the expense of his employer might do. Knowing that he has a business trip coming up, say to a conference where the dates are set in stone, the employee books a low-cost ticket, possibly involving a stopover, as they tend to be the least costly.

Then the employee watches the fares and when a particularly high fare to that location shows up, he books a seat on that flight also. He gets the receipt and then cancels the ticket. But, he has the important receipt and hopefully it will show up on his credit card statement. Ideally, from his point of view, the cancellation will show up on a different credit card statement. He takes the trip using the cheaper ticket but puts in for reimbursement using the receipt for the higher-cost ticket.

Catching this fraud—and I do think this is fraud—is not easy. For starters, require boarding passes for all reimbursed flights. Compare the flight number on the boarding pass with the flight number on the receipt for payment of the airline ticket. This is a lot of work and only a tiny fraction of travelers will try this fraud. So, you might only spot check on this item. Once you discover that someone has pulled this stunt, pull every travel report they have submitted and check them all.

If the employee submits only the credit card bill, it may reference only the flight location and a ticketing number. This may not give you the information you need. You can also require that the employee submit the booking receipt he received from the online booking service used. The flight number on the receipt should match the flight number on the boarding pass. Yes, he can submit the receipt for the more expensive flight, but the flight number won't match, unless it is for the same flight. Then check the booking number. This is a hard fraud to catch. Also, if he took a cheaper flight with a change required, the destinations on the boarding passes won't match.

ROGUE TRAVELERS

Most of your employees won't understand that taking the lowest rate found on the Internet may occasionally not be good for the company. Many companies routinely required employees to book their travel arrangements through preapproved travel agencies. Larger companies negotiate special rates, based on volume usage, with airlines, hotel chains, and car rental agencies. In the past, the employees had no way of knowing if there were lower rates available.

The Internet has changed a lot of this. Employees routinely surf the Internet, finding lower airfares and hotel rates than are being offered by the corporate plan. Until recently, the prevailing wisdom was to stick with the corporate rate because, overall, the company gained more, due largely to the volume discounts offered by such plans. That view is starting to change as some companies now allow employees to take advantage of these lower rates when they find them.

The first crack in the agency system has appeared as one of the *Fortune* 500 companies has moved completely to the Internet for domestic travel. The savings?—the $40 to $60 per ticket now previously paid to the agency. While this number has dropped dramatically, companies need to evaluate whether they are better off with their negotiated contracts or letting their employees search for the best rates.

If they decide that the negotiated rates are the best, then they need to make this clear to their employees. The policy regarding this should be spelled out in writing in the corporate T&E policy. There is no right or wrong answer to this question. It is just imperative that the company maximize its savings if it decides to go for the discounts.

Once it has been explained to employees that they are to use the preferred carriers, if possible, the policy needs to be enforced. Perhaps one violation might be tolerated with a note being sent to the employee explaining the overall benefits and instructing the employee that the next violation will not be reimbursed. The employee's boss should be copied on the warning as he or she is responsible for approving the expense report.

If it happens again, refuse to pay the expense, assuming management will back you up in this action. Otherwise, you are asking for trouble.

WHEN AN EMPLOYEE DEPARTS

Most of the issues in this section will apply to those companies who provide their employees with a T&E card. Employees should be instructed to turn in their card as part of their exit process. In fact, if Human Resources conducts an exit interview or goes through a process where it gets back keys and employee ID cards, it can be instructed to also get back the T&E card.

Otherwise, in a small percentage of cases, there will be a problem. This will occur when the employee uses the card for personal expenses. To a lesser extent the problem can occur if the employee was given a cash advance and never accounted for the funds, and/or perhaps never spent them on company business. As cash advances continue to become less common, the cash advance problem will become less and less of an issue.

For starters, as part of the T&E as well as the employee manual, employees should be told that T&E cards need to be returned to the company when they depart. They also need to be informed that it is expected that they will submit approved T&E reports for all company travel before they depart.

WHEN AN EMPLOYEE IS TERMINATED

All's fine and dandy when the parting is amicable, but occasionally it is not. Human Resources should inform Accounts Payable or whoever is responsible for the T&E card program whenever an employee is fired. The cards of departing employees, whether fired or leaving of their own volition, should be terminated immediately.

If there is an outstanding cash advance, the employee should be instructed to complete the T&E expense report or return the advance. To be perfectly candid about the matter, it is not likely that this issue is high on anyone's agenda at the time an employee is fired.

If the manager responsible for the card program suspects that Human Resources is not informing him when employees depart, request a list of active employees and run it against those who have cards. If any name is missing, immediately find out what happened and cancel those cards.

Additionally, if you find out after the fact, or perhaps through the rumor mill, that someone was let go, confirm the fact and then immediately request a copy of her recent charges. Even though the employee may be responsible for the bill, many companies have a secondary liability. Additionally, many feel a responsibility to pay the bill even if not legally required to do so if the employee neglects to pay it. This is often done to ensure that the bank will continue to offer cards to existing employees.

11

T&E Fraud: How to Prevent It

INTRODUCTION

The term *occupational fraud* is defined by the Association of Certified Fraud Examiners (ACFE) as: "The use of one's occupation for personal enrichment through the deliberate misuse or misapplication of the employing organization's resources or assets." As you might expect, expense reimbursement falls under the heading of occupational fraud.

REVIEW OF OCCUPATIONAL FRAUD

In its biannual *2006 Report to the Nation*, the ACFE reports that expense reimbursement ranked second in terms of frequency, but it had the lowest median loss at $25,000. Fraud tends to be committed by long-term, trusted employees. Adding insult to injury, the average losses increase with tenure. Of course, some of this makes sense, as the longer the employee is with an organization the longer he or she has to commit the fraud.

Who commits this fraud? Just over 30% of the perpetrators came from the accounting function with another 21% from upper management and the executive ranks. This latter group had much larger ill-gotten gains, with their average loss coming in at a whopping $900,000. Contrast this with the accounting group's smaller average losses of $199,000. You might be interested to know that the largest losses were attributable to purchasing.

For accounting, expense reimbursement fraud is the fifth most common methodology used to get their hands on funds that belong to their employer while it is the second most common approach for the executive group and the third most common technique used by the sales force to extract funds that don't belong to them.

While purchasing may have the largest losses, they are tied with internal audit for being the least likely to use expense reimbursement fraud.

IS EXPENSE REIMBURSEMENT REALLY A PROBLEM FOR THE AVERAGE COMPANY?

While these amounts are a bit mind numbing, you are probably wondering just how common travel and entertainment (T&E) fraud really is. To get an answer to that question, *Accounts Payable Now & Tomorrow* polled its readers and asked them about such frauds, instructing them to ignore small-dollar occurrences like a movie or drinks that were charged against policy.

While this is certainly not something to be overlooked, it is not in the same category as a large-dollar fraud. Even with these instructions, 38.03% of the respondents indicated that they had some T&E fraud in their organizations.

Any fraud numbers tend to understate the problem. For starters, some executives are too embarrassed to admit that this happened on their watch and will deny it happened. The fear of public ridicule is high and of special concern to those employed at publicly traded companies. Second, only frauds that have been uncovered can be reported. Frauds that are ongoing cannot.

Case Study: T&E Fraud

As part of the *Accounts Payable Now & Tomorrow* survey, readers were asked to share the details of their T&E fraud. Most felt they had stuck their necks out far enough just admitting that they had the fraud and were reluctant to share the details. Still, a number did so, and here's what they said:

- Not sure of the extent of it, but a former CFO was purchasing material items that were supposedly for clients.
- CEO was expensing personal items and trips. The IRS was involved and the CEO went to prison and paid fines/interest.
- Reimbursements for nonemployee spousal expenses were submitted. Trying to reimburse for personal-use rental cars while attending events where family was taken along as well. We've even had to get conference officials involved to prove the fraud.
- Employee had checks rerouted to an address in another state for payables vendors, non-T&E vendors.
- We did not have a policy, but because we did not have a policy we had very obvious abuse.
- Plane reservations made to accommodate visits with girlfriend in another state.
- Employee took customer on his boat and expected to be reimbursed for life jackets, skis, etc.
- It wasn't a large-dollar fraud but it was blatant. Two employees traveled to Las Vegas for a conference. They submitted

─────────── CASE STUDY: T&E FRAUD ───────────

meal receipts for parties of four rather than two. Their spouses accompanied them on the trip. Each employee was spoken to by their Director and the expense reports were adjusted for the additional meal expense.

- I discovered it in the only two cases we've had. The first employee complained so much about not being reimbursed, she quit. The second time it was an executive-level employee and it was "determined" that they didn't really mean to submit airfares that had already been paid for previously.

- Our system found some and other employees sometimes do. We have a reward for people turning others in.

- The individual also had a corporate purchasing card. He would not turn in all his receipts on his purchasing log but would instead submit them on his T&E. The company thus paid the expenses twice. This was discovered by accident. It was reported to Human Resources and Human Resources spoke to the employee and his supervisor. His purchasing card has been taken away.

- We had a manager who was taking his family out to eat on a regular basis and claiming it was customer entertainment. We caught it when we noticed the dates (weekends) and times on the receipts. The employee was terminated.

- Some former employees were buying personal items with the corporate card. They did not provide itemized receipts, which were required. They were reporting these items as company business expenses. Audits of expense reports found this.

- Movie was put on hotel bill. It was discovered in Accounts Payable when entering payment in system. Accounts Payable gave the employee a chance to pay and he didn't. The matter was forwarded to payroll, where it was deducted from the employee's paycheck. (Author's note: Unbelievable!)

- Production manager entertaining girlfriend on company card. Vice president checked on dates and times, which did not correspond to company business events. Manager was fired.

CASE STUDY: T&E FRAUD

- Discovered during the audit process. Employee was terminated and required to reimburse the company.
- Employee forged approver's signature. This was discovered when employee's total submitted expenses appeared on the list of top spenders in the company and that appearance was unexpected. The employee had electronically approved the expense reports using the manager's sign-on.
- We've had movies, drinks (which the company does not pay for), and cover charges submitted. After speaking with the department director, we have taken the charges off. This happens often enough for us to continue checking 100% of the reports.
- Employee had to reimburse company for "call girl service" in Las Vegas.
- Investigated by Loss Prevention Department. Terminated employee. Sometimes employee reimburses; if they don't, then charges are filed.
- Employee submitted item on expense report and vendor check request.
- We had an employee who declared $12,000 in a three-year period for bogus meals. He was caught due to becoming sloppy with his meal receipts, which were numbered. He began to submit them in numeric order. The employee was terminated. However, this occurred before automation.
- Conference in California, receipts from Florida and for different dates.

SCANNING FRAUD AND RECEIPTS

If you think you've now seen everything when it comes to expense reimbursement fraud, you haven't. InterplX's Chuck Buckner was showing a group of Accounts Payable professionals a sample fax and scanned receipts at a conference. He had one where an employee decided to modify a receipt to show a higher dollar amount. Since the employee couldn't line up the numbers correctly, he or she used typewriter eraser tape and correction fluid to enter a new dollar amount.

A really alert processor noticed a few minor odd-looking dashes on the scanned receipt and requested the original. Here comes what one of the attendees dubbed "that special kind of stupid." The employee sent the original receipt with all the correction fluid and tape into the processor.

WHERE EMPLOYEES LEARN HOW TO STEAL

I must be either a goody-two-shoes or completely naïve, because I am horrified by a book making the rounds, entitled *How to Pad Your Expense Report ... and Get Away With It!* Employee X (the author) provides tips to those who want to increase their income by illegally inflating their expense reports. I have read this slim book and made copious notes—on what companies and their Accounts Payable departments can do to ensure their employees do not employ the ruses suggested in this book. What follows is a look at some of the more egregious practices advocated, a list of signs you can look for on employee T&E reports that might signal a problem and some recommended best practices.

Danger Signs

Many of the strategies revolve around getting receipts. For example, employees booking airline trips themselves are advised to book several flights for the trip they will ultimately take. Once they have that coveted receipt for an expensive trip in hand, they can cancel that trip and book a less expensive one while submitting the receipt for the most expensive trip. Here are some of the things you should look for to help uncover possible fraud (and, yes, fraud is exactly what these strategies are):

- Sequential numbers on receipts, especially cash receipts. Compare several expense reports for the same employee if you suspect one.
- If there are more than occasional handwritten charge slips, take a closer look at the entire report.
- Too many cash receipts, especially if they look like adding machine tape, for low-cost meals.
- Double check the reports of employees traveling together to make sure that they are not both submitting for meal reimbursement for each other.
- Look really closely at the receipts for e-tickets. If you have the slightest doubt that the trip was taken, ask for the boarding passes. Of course, even this will not guard against the multiple-booking strategy discussed above.

Proceed carefully. Not everything that looks like a scam *is* a scam. Sometimes a handwritten receipt is legit. But a preponderance of these types of signs on one employee's reimbursement forms is generally a signal that further investigation is required. Let me point out something else: An employee who cheats regularly on his or her expense account is likely to have other problems. Many a corporate fraud has been uncovered because the individual involved got sloppy with expense reports.

Scams

In addition to the airfare scheme discussed earlier, a similar strategy can be used at hotels. Employees entitled to lower room rates, perhaps because of a convention or corporate rate, neglect to mention this when checking in. Then, after they've checked out and gotten that all-important receipt, they return to the front desk, make a fuss, and get charged the lower rate. And then, of course, they hold onto that first coveted invoice showing the higher rate.

Similar scams involve ordering foodservice in a hotel and then complaining and having it taken off the bill, taking a friend instead of a business client to dinner (because your boss will never check up with the client), submitting group receipts where the group members have already reimbursed you, and so on.

Drawing a Line

Dumpster diving is another practice advocated to get those sought-after receipts! How far is Employee X willing to go? Here's what he says: "Failing the above methods, there is always the old standby of going through the trash." He goes on to note that no one watches the trash, which is unfortunate because this is where most crooks get credit card numbers. You'll be happy to know he does not condone this practice. He writes, "For some strange reason, I don't see anything morally wrong with ripping off my company through expense reports, but using someone else's charge card number is not fair to fellow travelers."

There's another dishonest aspect to his practices that he never addresses, either. Many of his techniques revolve around bullying or harassing the clerks who work in the hotels and restaurants. Telling the room service staff that the food was poor when you actually enjoyed the meal is despicable.

DEALING WITH FRAUD: TWO EXTREMES

The following real-life examples represent two extremes at opposite ends of the spectrum of dealing with employee fraud. In the first, two lower-level supervisors went to a conference together. It was their first business trip. They noticed when they had dinner that there were several receipts provided by the restaurant. The two women returned from the trip and both put in for reimbursement using the same receipt. It was discovered and both women were fired.

In the second, a savvy Accounts Payable manager discovered that one of the company's salesmen had been inflating the mileage on his trips, collecting extra reimbursement for each trip. She went through his expense reports for the prior three years and determined that he had collected an extra $1,200 over that time period. He was presented with the facts and agreed with the conclusion. He agreed to make restitution under a payment plan. He made one payment and then stopped paying even though he was still employed by the company. The manager tried to get him to pay up, even copying his boss on her notes to him.

Finally in desperation, she put through a debit against future expense reimbursement requests and got the money that way. No action was taken against this employee.

T&E FRAUD PREVENTION BEST PRACTICES

So, what can you do to ensure that none of your employees ask for reimbursements that they are not entitled to? Here are some suggestions:

- Have a firm policy, endorsed by upper management, that makes it clear to all employees that cheating on an expense report will result in termination. We're not talking about someone who makes a small honest mistake. We are talking about the guy who pays $178 for a plane ticket but manages to come up with a receipt for $673 and asks for reimbursement for the larger amount.
- Use a corporate T&E card. Until I read the book, *How to Pad Your Expense Report ... and Get Away With It!*, I didn't think it was crucial other than for financial

cost-saving reasons. Any large company with more than a few employees leaves itself open to this type of fraud if they do not use one.

- If a corporate T&E card is not used, make it clear to employees that you have the right to see the credit card bills for the account they use for business events. When in doubt, ask for the credit card bill in question and the one for the following month. Sometimes, the dubious refunds will not show up until the following month.

- While we do not advocate thoroughly checking every expense report, randomly select a certain percentage each month and verify every last cent on that report. Make sure your travelers know this is done.

   ○ Should your suspicions be aroused regarding any one employee, put that individual's reports on the to-be-checked-thoroughly list each month.

   ○ Once a year, select a small number of employees who travel a lot and pull all their reports. Look at them in total. Does anything strike you as odd? Are there sequentially numbered receipts?

- Periodically send a traveler a note that says, "Congratulations! You have successfully passed your expense reimbursement audit," and let the rumor mill take care of the rest. This puts your employees on notice that checking of expense reports is going on even if their bosses never give the reports a second glance.

DETECTING EXPENSE REIMBURSEMENT FRAUD

Your processors should be suspicious and have the right to ask for additional documentation if they suspect something is not right. The example of the processor who was suspicious of the scanned receipt with those odd-looking marks is an example.

When spot checking expense reports, always check your known rogue spenders and make sure they know they are being monitored. Given the statistics above, always check your senior executives as well. Not only do they fall into the group more likely to commit expense reimbursement fraud, they also tend to spend the most money. This is a question of getting the most bang for your expense-review buck.

Your policy should require that the highest-ranking employee at an event pay for and submit for reimbursement when more than one employee is included in an event. Spot check your receipts closely when there is a large expenditure for entertainment to make sure that the manager approving the expense was not included in that entertainment.

Periodically, double check the mileage being submitted by travelers for reimbursement. Use one of the online mapping sites such as MapQuest. While the mileage won't be exact, it should be close.

WHAT TO DO WHEN EXPENSE REIMBURSEMENT FRAUD IS DETECTED

There is no right or wrong way to deal with this issue. The organization should have a policy for dealing with employee fraud and decide in advance what it is. Then it should be applied uniformly. If it is not, the organization could be opening itself up to all sorts of discrimination claims. Most organizations will give the employee the opportunity to make reimbursement if the dollar amount is small and it is a one-time offense. They take the view that it is an honest mistake; and that may very well be the case.

Others take a much firmer stance as in the earlier example of the two women caught submitting the same meal receipt and fire anyone who has been found guilty. The benefit of this stance is that if it is public it sets an example and serves as a deterrent to other employees. This does not mean that there needs to be an announcement, especially in the case of small dollars. However, by making sure that it is not kept a secret, most companies can rely on their ever-efficient rumor mill to get the word out.

The next issue revolves around whether to demand restitution and whether to prosecute. Even if restitution is demanded, few organizations ever get it and even fewer get 100% of what is owed.

Prosecution is a delicate issue. Many simply let the employee go and eat the loss, avoiding getting the police involved. They do not wish the public scrutiny that prosecution could bring. Not prosecuting leaves the employee free to go elsewhere and commit similar crimes, especially if he or she is under pressure to make restitution of a serious amount of money.

LAST-DITCH COLLECTION EFFORTS

While most employees who are caught in expense reimbursement fraud will agree to make restitution, getting those funds often turns out to be a bigger problem than anticipated. Before implementing the following suggestion, make sure you have senior management approval in writing, for this is bound to bring some loud complaints.

If the person involved is still employed by the company and restitution seems to be unlikely, add the amount to the person's W-2 at year-end, effectively turning it into taxable income. In a much publicized case involving the president of American University, the university was so outraged by his behavior that they retroactively corrected his W-2s for the amounts involved. More than one year was involved. The individual then had to deal with the IRS over taxes owed.

If the person involved is not employed by the company and restitution seems to be going nowhere, some have had success with reporting it on a 1099. If you use either of these approaches, make sure to discuss it with your tax professionals before taking action.

Perhaps just the threat of this might be enough to get the funds back.

GIFT CARD PROBLEM

On January 31, 2006, Tom Coughlin, a former Wal-Mart vice chairman, pleaded guilty to fraud involving the theft of money, gift cards, and merchandise from the retailer that employed him. He has been accused of misusing more than half a million dollars of company funds via fraudulent reimbursements. One of his tricks allegedly was to use gift cards intended for lower-ranking employees (to raise morale!) for personal expenses. His misdeeds do point to yet another area that Accounts Payable needs to monitor.

To be honest, this is not the first time we've heard tales of high-ranking employees taking gift cards meant for rank-and-filers. Does your organization use gift cards either in the manner Wal-Mart intended or for year-end rewards? What, if any, controls and/or audits are done to ensure the cards are used legitimately? We asked a group of Accounts Payable professionals for suggestions and they came up with a number of good ones.

NOT-PRETTY GIFT CARD SOLUTION

The first thing Accounts Payable can (and probably should) do is to raise the issue. Clearly, an Accounts Payable manager would not be in a position to question or audit the use of gift cards by a high-ranking executive without the formal backing of the organization's management. We do not think, in light of what has gone on, that it would be unreasonable to require that executives using these cards provide a list of recipients that can be spot checked to ensure proper use. Yes, this is definitely not a pretty solution but the problem itself is ugly.

Some other gift card approaches include:

- Use e-mail to distribute gift cards to intended recipients.
- Have gift cards controlled by the company's corporate Human Resources representative.
- Have employees sign for receipt of their certificate/card so you have documentation it indeed went to the appropriate person.
- Some form of acknowledgment in the form of an e-mail or interoffice memo, letter, and so forth could be used to inform the intended recipients of the reward. Include a simple note in the thank-you-for-your-work-efforts communication that if they have not received the card by a certain date to contact the sender. This alone should deter abusers or at least cause them some concern for being found out eventually. It should not be too difficult to ensure the number of cards issued correspond with the messages sent to recipients.

ALTERNATIVE TO GIFT CARDS

Recognizing the potential for abuse, more than one person suggested avoiding the cards completely. Here are two professionals' thoughts on this slant:

1. Instead of issuing loaded gift cards to employees, certificates that can be redeemed for gift cards can be given. This certificate would state the dollar amount of the gift card and have the signature of the employee who redeems

the gift card, as well as the signature of the person giving the gift card to the employee. An employee should be
responsible for loading all employee gift cards and should
verify the signatures before the gift card is issued. This
employee's supervisor should review the signed certificates on a regular basis, looking for any abnormalities (i.e.,
the same employee receiving multiple gift cards, etc.). As
a high-level control, executives can set a limit on supervisors' ability to issue gift card certificates, and this limit
can be used as a double check of gift cards issued.

2. Issue (redeemable at, say, Wal-Mart only) checks for the
    gift card amount (e.g., $100). Require endorsement on
    reverse side of check to include:
    ○ Signature
    ○ Printed name
    ○ Employee number

Examine the canceled checks when they come back to ensure
they agree to the company payroll list. While this approach does
not guarantee that they were used by Wal-Mart employees, you'd
get some idea of how many were or were not. At the register,
require verification of name with an employee ID card when
checks are tendered.

12

AUTOMATION: THIRD-PARTY AND HOME-GROWN SYSTEMS

INTRODUCTION

This chapter explores third-party and home-grown automation systems such as:

- Excel versus the rest (Gelco, InterplX, Concur, expensewatch, etc.)
- Amex
- Runzheimer

Automation of the travel and entertainment (T&E) reporting, approval, review, and reimbursement process effectively ends many of the problems discussed elsewhere in this book. However, as you will see in the numbers provided in the following section, not many organizations have taken that step. Often they were simply not willing to spend the money needed to get the software, although that is changing with the development of pay-as-you-go models.

Many organizations still rely on Excel-based models, mostly developed in-house. While this is a great step, especially for those previously using a handwritten form, it is not what we mean when we discuss an automated process. However, given the level of travel within your organization, it may be perfectly adequate.

HOW T&E EXPENSES ARE REPORTED

There are several good T&E software programs and ASP models on the market today. But, few companies use them, the majority preferring, it seems, to rely on simple programs developed in-house in Excel. And to be perfectly honest, the Excel models do an adequate job given the cost, although they do not have the functionality that is incorporated into some of the fancier models.

To find out exactly how the corporate world is handling their T&E expenditures, *Accounts Payable Now & Tomorrow* surveyed its readers. Here's what they reported:

On a handwritten form	16.67%
On a form based on Excel	45.83%
Online, using an ASP model	15.28%
Other	22.22%

EXCEL-BASED MODELS

Without a doubt, you can't beat the price of T&E expense reports based on Excel. They are either free, if you overlook your own in-house development costs, or modestly priced if you used something like Shortcuts to Expense Reports, which is currently priced at a whopping $17 (www.panache-yes.com/learn_expensereports.html).

All Excel models—whether purchased or in-house-developed models—should have the formulas locked to prevent cheating employees from playing games. If the formulas are not locked, you are back to square one when it comes to verifying the data. Without locked formulas you will need to check the calculations on reports to detect whether changes have been made where they shouldn't have been made.

Here's what Excel models don't provide:

- Automated contract compliance
- Ability to aggregate data for negotiation and budgeting purposes
- Ability to highlight contract exceptions
- Automated escalation for approvals

While these models are still attractive from a cost standpoint, many organizations, as noted elsewhere in the book, are cleaning up their T&E reimbursement process thanks to the passage of the Sarbanes-Oxley Act. This is especially true of public companies that need to demonstrate strong internal controls, which their prior processes often lacked. Thus, there is some move away from Excel models to ASP models that contain nifty control and monitoring features.

WHY AUTOMATE?

Automation takes human error out of the equation. With a computer doing the calculations instead of your employees and a calculator, mathematical errors disappear. This also means you don't have to waste valuable human resources on a clerical task. Additional benefits include:

- Faster employee reimbursement of out-of-pocket expenses, which in turn improves employee satisfaction with the T&E program
- Prepopulation of the employees' expense report forms with data from the corporate credit card, again making the process a little easier for employees
- Ability to capture data for budgeting and negotiation purposes
- Automated policy compliance reviews
- Ability to escalate employee expense reports for approval if that is desired

The timely reimbursements that are possible with such a system have made it possible for many companies to eliminate some or all of the cash advances for those who travel. Not only is this a financial savings for the company, it is a process improvement to the entire T&E function.

There is an often-hidden cost savings associated with automation. Although few employees will admit this publicly, many of them use their organization's overnight mail service to send in their T&E expense reports and receipts to the area responsible for processing, especially if the deadlines for their credit card payments are nearing. This is a very expensive way to submit reports.

Moreover, some compassionate Accounts Payable staffs, understanding the pressures on employees, will send the reimbursement checks back the same way. Even if the organization has negotiated an attractive rate with the overnight carrier, this is still an added expense that rarely gets included in the calculation of the total costs associated with T&E expense reporting and reimbursement. Needless to say, it is more cost effective and efficient to have the reports submitted electronically and the reimbursements done through an electronic deposit to a bank account designated by the employee.

It is an unfortunate fact of corporate life that a few employees will try to cheat their employers. As discussed in Chapter 11, fraud on employees' T&E reports happens more than most of us would like to admit. Use of an automated process makes it a little more difficult to commit such fraud.

Finally, the systems allow a more efficient use of the AP department's resources, permitting the staff to focus on more productive work rather than spending their time on clerical processes often associated with the T&E review and reimbursement function. By making the process more palatable to traveling employees, you will also lessen the negative interactions with Accounts Payable when there are payment timing disputes, compliance issues, and delayed approvals.

HOW AUTOMATED SYSTEMS WORK: OVERVIEW

Speaking at IRSCompliance.org's conference, Chuck Buckner, president and CEO of InterplX Technologies, provided a thorough explanation of the functionality of most of the automated systems on the market today. They are designed to create, submit, and approve an expense claim through the following process:

Step 1: Data is imported from the charge card company and the employees' expense reports are prepopulated with that data. Although some companies also import information from travel agencies, there is a debate on that issue. The reason is that approximately 30% of business trips are changed after the traveler has begun the trip. Hence, including this data can lead to many corrections.

Step 2: The employee adds his or her out-of-pocket expenses. Depending on the system, this can be done either at the completion of the trip or throughout the trip.

Step 3: Coding information and other data are added. Where the general ledger (GL) coding is done is a decision that needs to be made at each organization, although many feel that it should be done by the traveler rather than Accounts Payable. By having the traveler do it there can be no issue of getting items coded to the wrong category. The downside of this is some enterprising travelers will code an item to a budget code that has money left in it, not the one where it belongs. Some organizations have the field code their line items but have it verified in Accounts Payable to guard against improper coding to match funding. Again, this is an issue that each organization will have to address on its own.

Step 4: Submit supporting documentation, namely the receipts and hotel folios. Most frequently the receipts are sent directly to Accounts Payable, bypassing the approving manager.

Step 5: The report is sent to the supervisor of the traveler for approval. It is an openly discussed issue among expense reporting professionals that most managers do not review the reports but merely sign them. This is part of the reason some of the new systems bypass the manager when it comes to receipts. However, some of the models provide the ability for the managers to view receipts online, if they so desire.

Step 6: The final approved report is forwarded to Accounts Payable for processing.

Buckner notes that there has been a strong move to web-based systems. Essentially these are centralized databases that provide visibility of information to all who need to see it—and with the proper controls, no one else.

AUTOMATED SYSTEMS: DESIGN REQUIREMENTS

At this same event, Buckner also described what he calls key design requirements for automated systems. He says most on the market today have these:

- Simple interfaces that reduce training requirements. If the systems are too complicated, your travelers will not use them. Since in most organizations the big travelers are the sales force, make sure it is easy enough for a person without a lot of patience for technology to use.
- Policy guidelines built in to help with compliance issues.
- Flexibility in workflow. After the passage of Sarbanes-Oxley, some organizations will allow payment only after the report has been approved.
- Integrated receipt management so that receipts are included but do not take over the process. The following section will discuss some of the automated alternatives currently available.
- E-mail notifications and reminders throughout the process so everyone involved knows where the report is and appropriate action can be taken if someone falls down on the job or is out of the office.
- Complete accounting integrations.
- Visibility (including policy exceptions) and metrics to help negotiating with preferred suppliers and for budget purposes.
- SAS Type II certification. This is the certification required for outsourced processes to ensure compliance with the Sarbanes-Oxley Act. There is a brief discussion below of this issue.
- International VAT (value-added tax) processing. This issue will be discussed in depth in Chapter 13. The best

automated systems provide their clients with a means to collect the data needed to reclaim VAT.

RECEIPTS IN AN AUTOMATED ENVIRONMENT

There are no two ways about it. You need the receipts. In an automated environment, receipts are submitted separately from the report itself. Most companies will not reimburse the employee until both the approved report and the receipts are received. A few will reimburse on the basis of the report and give the employee some number of days to submit the receipts. This should be addressed in the policy, taking into account IRS guidelines. There are several ways to handle receipts:

- Faxing receipts in from the locations to the Accounts Payable group usually includes using a cover sheet that either has a unique assigned number on it that will ultimately match the receipts with the expense report in question or is bar coded with the appropriate information. Occasionally employees will not realize the importance of the cover sheet and will try to fax receipts with their own made-up cover sheet. Thus, the importance of the cover sheet needs to be fully explained.
- Receipts are scanned locally and sent to Accounts Payable for processing. Again, the cover sheet with the unique identifier or bar codes needs to be included. Buckner suggests that this is the best way to handle receipts.
- Receipts can be scanned centrally, but this requires a double process as the employee has to send the receipts and then someone has to open the envelope, scan the receipts, and match to the report. It can become a debate as to who lost a receipt when one is missing.

- Receipts are not imaged and sent in on paper. This is a real option used by a number of companies that do not think the cost involved in imaging is worth it, given the dollar amount of most receipts.

Note that if either of the first two options is selected (the faxing or the local scanning), employees should hold onto the receipts for as long as the company policy mandates. This may be a few days, 90 days, or in rare instances, 7 years. The reason for this is there may be a need to see the original receipt. As you may remember, in Chapter 11, one potential embezzlement was discovered when an employee processing a scanned T&E receipt requested the original. You should instruct your employees to hold onto receipts for as long as you feel it necessary to complete your reviews.

Note also that technology isn't perfect, especially when working with receipts that are of questionable quality. Thus, your processors may need to request original receipts not only because they may suspect tampering but also because the scanning or faxing resulted in blurred data.

REIMBURSEMENT PAYMENTS IN AN AUTOMATED ENVIRONMENT

Automated systems not only make employee reimbursements more timely, they offer additional flexibility. Most will allow payment through the payment option that is most cost effective to the organization: the automated clearinghouse (ACH) credit, like the direct deposit of payroll. In fact, a few organizations will include payment for T&E reimbursement with their payroll.

Buckner also says that automated systems:

- Offer flexibility on timing when it comes to payments.

- Have the ability to split a payment with one part going to the corporate card and another to a bank designated by the employee (which may be different from the account where payroll is deposited).
- Provide reconciliation support.
- Can be integrated with the GL so it is updated when the payment is made.
- Send out automated payment notifications so employees know when money has been deposited in their accounts and when their credit card provider has been paid.

COMPANIES OFFERING T&E AUTOMATED SERVICES

This is a space that is rapidly changing. As new functionality becomes popular, savvy service providers are adapting their systems to meet market demand. Some of the big enterprise resource planning (ERP) systems have T&E modules, including SAP, Microsoft, and Oracle. So before spending money on third-party software and then having to have your IT staff work on the integration, check to see if you already have the capability in your existing software and what it will take to get it up and running.

It should be noted that some organizations that do have the capabilities in their ERP system still choose to purchase a third-party solution as it better meets their unique requirements.

Here are a few companies who are currently in the automated T&E space (listed in alphabetical order):

- Basware
- Concur Technologies
- Expensewatch
- Gelco

- InterplX Technologies
- Necho Systems
- Runzheimer

The lines are blurring as companies like GEAC and Ariba offer products that can be used for T&E as part of their other offerings and spend management initiatives. Each of these organizations has a presence on the Web and readers can investigate the pros and cons of each.

SARBANES-OXLEY ACT AND OUTSOURCED OPERATIONS

Under Sarbanes-Oxley, management is responsible for evaluating the design and effectiveness of the control structure in place both within the third-party provider and between the two organizations if an outsourcer is used and it directly impacts the financial reporting or internal control environment activities. So, you can see that the control requirements do not completely go away simply by outsourcing the function.

Practically speaking, companies that outsource their T&E function now have to address two additional issues if they are to be Sarbanes-Oxley compliant:

1. The determination of outsourcing with regard to impacting financial reporting
2. The identification of the most appropriate mechanism for demonstrating effective controls on outsourced functions

The Securities and Exchange Commission (SEC) stepped into the fray and provided a solution. After reviewing Section 404 requirements and interpreting them as they pertain to outsourced operations, the SEC provided a resolution. In June 2004, the SEC announced that companies relying on third-party service providers could rely on Type II SAS 70 reports to assess the internal controls in those operations.

SAS 70

The Statement on Auditing Standards for service organizations (SAS 70) was developed by the American Institute of Certified Public Accountants (AICPA). An SAS 70 audit (sometimes called *service auditor's examination*) verifies that the control objectives and activities of the subject company are in place. At the end of the examination, assuming that the appropriate controls are in place, a formal report is issued to the service provider.

This SAS 70 report, often referred to as the *Service Auditor's Report,* is given to auditors at companies using the services of the outsourcer to permit them to certify the controls of their clients. There are two types of reports, referred to as Type I and Type II.

Both Type I and Type II reports include:

- Independent Service Auditor's Report
- Service organization's description of controls

Type I reports include:

- Several optional features such as:
  - A description of the service auditor's tests of operating effectiveness and the results of those tests. This information is provided by the independent service auditor.
  - Other information the service organization chooses to include.

The Type I report describes the controls in place at a specific point in time. In this report the service auditor will offer its opinion on whether the description of its controls fairly presents the relevant aspects of the organization's controls and whether the controls were designed appropriately to achieve the specified control objectives.

Type II reports include:

- A description of the service auditor's test of operating effectiveness and the results of those tests. This information is provided by the independent service auditor.
- Other information the service organization chooses to provide.

The Type II report is not for a specified point in time, but rather includes detailed testing of the service organization's controls over a minimum six-month period.

In addition to the items certified in the Type I report, the Type II reports include an opinion as to whether the controls tested were operating with sufficient effectiveness to provide reasonable assurance that control objectives were achieved during the specified period. The important feature to note here is the use of the word *reasonable*. The report does not guarantee that the control objectives have been achieved but rather that there is a reasonable certainty that the objectives have been achieved.

The SEC has deemed the Type II report appropriate for companies using third-party service providers to rely on.

13

PERTINENT ISSUES FOR INTERNATIONAL TRAVELERS

INTRODUCTION

Your international travelers face a host of issues not faced by employees who travel domestically. International travel bills, if handled correctly, also offer an opportunity for organizations to get some of their funds back through VAT (value-added tax) reclaim. Before delving into that topic in detail, we'll take a look at a few other issues affecting international travel.

BRIBES

The answer here to employees considering giving a bribe should be a resounding *no*. The reason is simple: It is illegal.

The Foreign Corrupt Practices Act specifically prohibits corrupt payments to foreign officials for the purpose of obtaining or keeping business. It applies to *any* individual, firm, officer, director, employee, or agent of a firm, and any stockholder acting on behalf of a firm. It also prohibits corrupt payments through intermediaries.

There is only one exception. The Act contains an explicit exception to the bribery prohibition for "facilitating payments" for "routine governmental action" and provides affirmative defenses that can be used to defend against alleged violations of the Foreign Corrupt Practices Act.

For additional information about the Act, visit the Department of Justice's web site at http://www.usdoj.gov/criminal/fraud/fcpa/dojdocb.htm.

FOREIGN EXCHANGE

When your employees travel internationally, the odds are high that they will require currency other than U.S. dollars. It is also likely that their expenses will be paid in that foreign currency although the credit card companies will convert those expenses to U.S. dollars.

The issue for the Accounts Payable staff reviewing the reports is the out-of-pocket expenses. They can check the conversion used by the employee on sites such as http://www.oanda.com/converter/classic. However, they need to keep something in mind.

For the most part, foreign exchange fluctuates continually. The exchange rate this morning will be different from the exchange rate this afternoon and definitely different from the rate last week. This is also an area where employees are likely to make mistakes. There is more than one way to handle this:

- Check the rate used by the traveler online and as long as it is somewhat close to the rate used, accept the employee's numbers. Make sure you use a site aimed at consumers and not one aimed at large corporate traders. The spreads on the consumer sites are apt to be large and, unfortunately, that is the rate your travelers will get. After all, the B2B rates are for million-dollar transactions and your travelers should not need that much cash. You will run into the same issue if you use rates published in sources like the *Wall Street Journal*.

- When your traveler exchanged money, he or she received a receipt showing the exchange rate plus any fees charged. Require that your traveler turn in this receipt to document the exchange rate. If this is a requirement, make sure your international travelers are aware of it. Otherwise, they are likely to throw this receipt away.

FOREIGN EXCHANGE TIPS

You might also suggest that travelers convert most, if not all, of their money at one time. The reason for this is that there is usually a flat fee charged each time money is exchanged. Better to pay this fee once than several times.

Additionally, travelers will get the best exchange rate in most currencies if they wait until they arrive in the foreign country. They can go either to one of the exchanges in the big cities or to a local bank.

They should avoid exchanging money at the airport, right after getting off the plane. Typically these places have a captive audience and do not offer attractive exchange rates. However, if the traveler needs to pay for a cab, he or she may have to exchange $100 or so.

Finally, this issue needs to be kept in perspective. While there are some tricks to getting the most attractive exchange rates, if your traveler has limited time and pressing business, it might be best to purchase the foreign exchange prior to the trip.

INTERNATIONAL TRAVEL ADVISORIES

Depending on the nature of your business and where your international travelers are going, they may need to be aware of government travel advisories. This information can be accessed at http://travel.state.gov/index.html.

VALUE-ADDED TAX

In many parts of the world, there is a tax added to the cost of goods and sometimes services. It is referred to as a value-added tax (VAT). Unlike our sales tax, VAT may be reclaimed under the right circumstances. This pertains to U.S. travelers to other countries, principally Europe and Canada. They are eligible to reclaim certain taxes they paid while traveling abroad.

Generally, these taxes are paid as part of various bills, such as hotel, conference charges, and so on. That said, reclaiming these amounts is not simple. Some companies are not even aware that they are entitled to get this money back, and others have no idea how to go about doing so.

What is reclaimable varies by country, and the rules for doing so are not consistent. Needless to say, the instructions are not very clear. Anyone who has ever tried to collect VAT payments made while traveling overseas knows that it can be a frustrating, paper-intensive, and annoying process. Many get so discouraged, they give up and never claim the money they are entitled to—which might be what the VAT authorities had in mind when they made the process so difficult.

However, if you wish to obtain a refund, an original invoice, together with an application form and other supporting documentation, must be submitted to the VAT authorities in the country where the expenditure was incurred.

In theory, this sounds simple enough, but it is not. Different countries have different rates; moreover, the VAT is recoverable on different items in different countries. Complicating the matter even further, especially for U.S. organizations, is the fact that the applications for the refund must be completed in the language of the country.

Unless you have a tremendous amount of international travel and have hired your own in-house expert, this is a function you will probably want to outsource. There are a number of organizations willing and able to help. Here are a few:

- Corporate VAT Management at www.autovat.com
- Meridian at www.meridianvat.com
- VAT Recovery Group at www.vrg.biz

Operational Issues

In addition to the onerous language constraint previously mentioned, those interested in reclaiming their VAT need to:

- Be aware of the deadlines for each country.
- Make sure their travelers bring back their original invoices.
- Make sure those invoices are made out in the company name and not the name of the traveling individual.
- Be aware of what's reclaimable in each country.

While the world may be going paperless, the VAT authorities are not there yet. The original invoice, which is the document that travelers receive when checking out of the hotel, is the source document. Copies won't do and neither will credit card receipts.

Is VAT an Issue for You?

John Powell, president of Corporate VAT Management, was asked how an organization could tell if it was worth pursuing the reclaim of its VAT. He suggests that organizations should be reclaiming:

- 3 to 5% of their international ground spend in Europe. This excludes airfare.
- 10% across the board in Australia once certain thresholds have been reached. Remember, do not include airfare.
- 7% in Canada, and the reclaim is pretty easy.

These basic calculations will tell you whether VAT reclaim is an issue you need to pursue. Let's face it, if your numbers show that you have a potential exposure of $10,000 or even $20,000, it probably will not be worth pursuing. Your company will spend more of its human and financial resources pursuing the reclaim than it will receive back.

Powell also notes that while the 80/20 rule might apply in most circumstances, when it comes to VAT reclaim, it's more like 95/5. That's right, 95% of your financial return will come from just 5% of your reports.

PAPERLESS T&E WORLD

While you may pursue paperless transactions everywhere else, when it comes to VAT reclaim, paperless is a terrible idea. VAT authorities simply will not recognize anything but the original invoice. But don't give up if you have already gone paperless. You or your outsourcer can use this data to request a *copy of the original invoice* from the hotels in question. While not perfect, invoices marked "Copy of original invoice for VAT refund" or something like that will work in most circumstances.

Information invoices and invoices made out in the traveler's name will not work. If you instruct your employees to do only one thing in this regard, it should be to ask the hotels to make out the invoices in the name of your organization, not their name. Thus the bill should be made out to ABC Company, not Jane Smith. This is contrary to what most people in North America expect, so the point needs to be drilled home to international travelers. Otherwise, there will be no VAT reclaim.

MAXIMIZING YOUR RETURNS

Remember the 95/5 rule discussed earlier. Apply that to your own situation. Powell advocates taking a "smart" approach. Dumb systems, he says, can hurt. They will flag all international expenses for research when in fact only a few of those items will actually contain VAT that is reclaimable or that is worth reclaiming.

Smart systems will focus on the larger items, allowing the professional responsible for VAT reclaim to go after those items. Those items will vary from organization to organization depending on the nature of your travel. For example, if experience shows that most of your VAT reclaim comes from hotel stays in two countries, then flag only those items. Don't bother with the potential reclaim for one country if the dollar amount is small, say $28.

Powell suggests making VAT recovery and the associated documents a requirement when negotiating for a preferred supplier.

He also notes, ever so tactfully, that reciprocity has become an issue with certain VAT authorities, some of whom view the U.S. sales tax as comparable. As you are probably well aware, the United States does not rebate sales tax to travelers from other countries; hence the issue. Northern European countries and Canada are probably the most VAT friendly. Note that in Canada, the tax in question is the Goods and Service Tax (GST).

Here are a few pointers to take into account when preparing your VAT reclaim:

- VAT on hotels is not reclaimable in France.
- VAT officials in the Netherlands are sticklers on the details.
- If you prepare your own returns, do not expect to get it right the first time. Your returns will be returned to you for correction. Handle them promptly given the deadlines.
- Focus on the areas where you will receive the largest refunds and ignore the rest. It will cost you more to handle the smaller refunds than the return is worth.

SARBANES-OXLEY

This is another area that has gotten increased scrutiny thanks to the scandals at Enron and WorldCom, among others. The passage of the Sarbanes-Oxley Act has caused a number of organizations to rethink the way they handle their whole T&E function. That review has enlightened a number of these organizations to the fact that they are passing up on potential VAT reclaim. This does not demonstrate great financial controls and so many are now, often for the first time, focusing on this issue. In fact, Powell estimates that only 20 to 30% of what is eligible for reclaim is being reclaimed. Of course, some of this is stuff that is too small to be bothered with, but most of it is not.

OUTSOURCERS

The organizations that know how to reclaim their VAT payments on their own are few and far between. Most need help. There are a number of issues that cause difficulty. They include:

- The detailed nature of the returns
- The need to have them in the native language of the country from which the VAT is being reclaimed
- The differing deadlines from country to country
- The different tariffs
- The fact that VAT is reclaimable on different items in different countries

DO-IT-YOURSELF VAT RECOVERY

Some reading this may be wondering whether they can handle their VAT recovery themselves or whether they should hire a third party to do it for them. Assuming there is adequate volume in countries where language is not an issue, it might be worthwhile.

Powell suggests that it is feasible to handle reclaims in both the United Kingdom and Canada. The forms are online and can be downloaded, and once you understand how to complete them it is possible to do it on an ongoing basis. Be aware that:

- This is very detail-oriented work.
- If the responsible person leaves, you will need to train someone else.
- You need to be conscious of the deadlines for each country.
- The work needs to be centrally organized as the number of claims per country allowable each reporting period is extremely limited.

Appendix B contains a chart that shows the current deadlines and requirements for many countries that permit VAT reclaim. These can change, so be sure to double check with the country in question before getting started. Note that VAT reclaim is available in many other locales, including Japan, Australia, and some eastern European countries. If you have sufficient activity in those locales, you might want to investigate the issue further.

Powell also notes that this function is usually handled in the travel department if the organization is large enough to have one. However, inevitably, assistance is needed from the Accounts Payable group when it comes to documentation, as proper documentation is sometimes lacking.

14

NEGOTIATING THE BEST RATE FROM SUPPLIERS

INTRODUCTION

Those professionals reading this who have a significant budget for travel and entertainment (T&E)
will want to look for ways to reduce those expenditures. Let's face it, if you have a significant
number of travelers, even a small reduction in
price can result in substantial bottom-line savings.
Every dollar saved on travel is a dollar added to
the bottom line. Thus controlling costs—always
a challenge—becomes crucial when it comes
to T&E.

One way to do this, of course, is through the use
of per diems and other limits, such as no first-class
travel. Another way to do this, if there is sufficient
travel, is to negotiate reduced rates with suppliers

for use of their services. Most suppliers are happy to do this, especially if it means there will be increased volume.

Keep in mind that you could have four types of suppliers:

1. Airlines
2. Lodging
3. Car rental
4. Credit card issuer

Don't overlook the fourth item when looking to cut costs on your travel. The credit card scenario sometimes offers organizations the opportunity for rebates, which some think is even better than reduced costs. Credit card issues are discussed at the end of this chapter.

THE BASICS

Rather than negotiate with every airline, for example, organizations have quickly learned that if they pooled their activity, demonstrating larger volume, they would get a better rate. After negotiating this lower rate, they have to deliver the travelers.

This means dictating to employees which airlines and which hotels they must stay in when traveling on company business. Be aware that it will lead to grumbling, because no matter what service provider you choose, a small portion of your employees will always prefer the competitor. Thus the issue unfortunately becomes one of demanding rather than suggesting. Left to their own devices, your employees will travel on airlines other than the preferred one and stay in hotels other than the preferred one.

Because of this and because not all service providers have locations in all the places an organization will need to travel, some companies will negotiate with two or three service providers. This assumes that the company has the volume to warrant more than one service provider for the particular service in question.

A MATTER OF POLICY

The organization will need to decide what the ramifications are for employees who neglect or refuse to use the preferred service provider. This is a matter of corporate culture and also a question of how far an organization is willing to push on this issue.

Some refuse to pay for accommodations or services used on any but the preferred provider unless provisions were made in advance. Others give employees one shot to make an error in this arena. Still others allow some discretion. They might sanction employees staying in a hotel if a conference was housed there, for example. Or they might approve a stay in a hotel that was not the preferred supplier if the nearest one was more than five or ten (or whatever is stipulated) miles from the meeting.

There is no right or wrong answer to this question. It should be addressed in the policy and all employees should be treated equally on this issue.

Finally, realize that the more employees are allowed to use other service providers, regardless of the reason, the less effective the negotiated rate is likely to be.

WHERE DO YOUR TRAVEL DOLLARS GO?

Before harnessing your efforts to begin negotiating with your travel suppliers, figure out where most of your travel dollars are spent. After all, it is a waste of time to negotiate with an airline if most of your employees travel by automobile. In that case, if they are renting cars, you might want to start with the car rental agencies.

If yours is like the "average" organization, you will have the biggest chunk of your spend going to air travel. Typically, this can account for 40 to 45% of a business traveler's expenditures. The second largest expenditure for a typical organization is lodging, with 20 to 25% of the travel dollars going to hotels. Finally, in most places, automobile rentals account for less than 10% of the budget.

But your organization may not be typical, so before you can start your negotiations, you will need to get your figures together. The information, if at all possible, should be broken down several ways. For starters, you should know how much you spent in each category in the last year or two. For the most part, this will be in the three major areas:

1. Airfare
2. Hotels
3. Car rentals

You would be surprised to learn how many organizations go into a negotiation without this information. In addition, the data should be further broken down into how much you spent with each service provider. For example, with airfare, break the data down further so you can see how much was spent with American, how much with Delta, how much with Continental, and so on.

This information will help you in two ways. First, you will be able to use it to negotiate better rates when the airlines see the volume you can deliver. Second, if they are not negotiating in good faith, you can also use the data to show them how much they will lose if they do not treat your organization correctly.

Although getting this information together before your negotiations may seem intuitive, many neglect this step. Depending on your systems, it may not be as easy to get this data together as you might hope. It may have to be pieced together from several places. Your credit card provider may be able to provide some of the information if you use a company-sponsored credit card.

Do not underestimate the time it will take to compile all the information. Ask for the data well in advance of the time when it is needed or you may find yourself negotiating without it.

Once you have this information and can combine it with your proposed travel budget for the upcoming year, you will be armed with the information you need to begin your negotiations.

ALL TRAVEL ON A COMPANY CARD

Compiling the spend for the prior year can be a real challenge if all travel charges are not put on one card. That's why some experts strongly recommend that organizations use a company-sponsored credit card and all travel-related charges be put on that card. This is especially easy if the card issuer can capture what is referred to as Level 3 data. Level 3 data includes Level 1 data (the date, supplier, and dollar amount), Level 2 data (sales tax and a variable data field), and item product code, description, quantity, unit of measure, price, and tax.

This makes it relatively easy to compile the data needed for negotiations. It also makes it easy to see who is not complying with the request to use preferred service providers and to have a conversation with them regarding this.

FOCUS ON YOUR BIGGEST SAVINGS

Once you've identified your largest concentration of spend, focus your efforts on negotiating with that supplier. But be aware that even though your largest dollars may be in airfare, most experts suggest that this is not the best place to start.

The conventional wisdom at this point in time suggests that you turn your negotiation efforts first to hotel bills. This assumes, of course, that your travelers spend the night away from home. The reason for this is that there generally are bigger savings to be had in lodging than in airfares. Additionally, you will have greater leverage there than with the airlines.

DON'T OVERLOOK INTERNATIONAL TRAVEL

When negotiating, many organizations focus only on their domestic spend. While international trips will probably not be as frequent as domestic travel, the dollars involved usually will be much higher. Make sure you include both, as it will give you more negotiating clout if the service providers in question have facilities in the countries where your international travel takes place.

If your preferred service providers do not offer service to the international locations where your travelers most frequently need to go, you may need to negotiate separately with service providers who offer the services you need in those locations.

THE CONTRACT IS NOT SET IN STONE

Occasionally conditions occurring in the marketplace change the dynamics of travel. The best example that comes to mind was the terrorist attacks in 2001 on the Pentagon and the World Trade Center towers. Business travel dropped dramatically. Some companies forbade corporate travel completely, while others allowed it only under special circumstances with special permission. Hotels and airlines scrambled to fill planes and rooms.

This provided a unique opportunity for those organizations whose employees were still traveling. Many of them were hurting financially and looked for ways to cut costs. Clearly, the travel budget was on the table. Some of them went back and successfully reopened the negotiations of their travel contracts with preferred suppliers. The burst of the dot-com bubble led to a similar, albeit less-publicized, situation.

A recession could provide the same opportunity in the future as could anything that temporarily keeps people from flying. The hotel industry could do it to itself if there is a boom in building and an oversupply of rooms.

DON'T PROMISE ALL YOUR BUSINESS

After you run your numbers it might be tempting to promise all business in the upcoming year to a particular airline or hotel chain to get the lowest rate. Resist the temptation. There are several reasons for this. For starters, you will be working off projected numbers. No one knows exactly what the final numbers will be until the year is completed.

Additionally, there are reasons why the preferred service providers do not always get used. In the case of hotels:

- They may not have a location that is convenient for a particular trip.
- If conferences are involved, employees usually like to stay in the hotel that is housing the conference.
- Occasionally a senior executive does not like the hotel chain and will choose to stay elsewhere. While this is really not right, it is rare that anyone will take him or her to task for this.

In the case of airlines:

- They may not have a route to a particular city.
- They may not offer a direct flight to a particular city.
- They may not have a flight that is convenient for a particular traveler.

- The flight that your traveler wants may be overbooked.
- A senior executive may prefer to fly on a different airline and no one is willing to take him or her to task over this.

OVERLOOKED T&E SAVINGS OPPORTUNITY

Many executives are so busy trying to negotiate a deal with the airlines, hotel chains, and car rental agencies that they overlook another potential arena for savings. In this case it is their T&E credit card given to their employees.

The traditional recommendation is to combine T&E spending on the corporate procurement card to increase the volume and hence the rebate the organization earns. This is not a bad idea. However, some firms have been reluctant to pursue this route as they do not wish to take on the liability for their employees' purchases. This is a real issue in those organizations that have a corporate card with employee pay and/or liability.

These firms have started to negotiate rebates from their T&E card issuers. While generally not as lucrative as when the spend is combined on the procurement card in a one-card-type arrangement, there are still rebate opportunities for those who wish to keep the T&E spending separate. This issue should be raised with the card issuer at the time the program is initiated or when it comes up for renewal. It can provide an additional savings. If your card issuer does not offer rebates, shop around until you find one that does.

When negotiating with your card issuer, talk about your payment dates with regard to the rebates. In addition to offering higher rebates for increased volume, some card issuers will also offer rebates for earlier payment dates. If your organization is in a cash-positive position, this should definitely be investigated (for your T&E card, your procurement card, and any one-card programs you may have).

Even if your organization is in a net borrowing position, you might want to investigate the rebates available for earlier payments. When you get the figures for both a normal payment date and an early payment date, compare this with your borrowing rate to determine if there is an arbitrage opportunity. If you have the ability to borrow at low rates, you may be able to add a few dollars to your organization's bottom line.

OTHER SAVINGS ASSOCIATED WITH YOUR T&E CARD

Look askance at any card issuer that asks for fees associated with issuing individual cards to your employees. While this was commonplace years ago, it is not today. Only the very smallest organizations with minimal volume on their cards should even have to address this issue. Sometimes all it takes is asking to have the fees waived.

Increasing the Rebate

It was only a few short years ago that organizations, often at the behest of their card issuers, were reluctant to discuss rebates in public. Those days are gone and today companies openly talk about ways to increase their rebates. A couple of items are emerging in this arena, items that once would never have been included. Both are employee expenses that are submitted for review and reimbursement. Hence some organizations feel they belong on the T&E card or a one card. They are tuition reimbursement and employee moving expenses.

Since both these items tend to be large dollars, it is easy to see why organizations would want to include them in their programs.

It should be noted that some universities are moving away from accepting tuition on credit cards. If your employees are attending such a university, that opportunity will not be available to you.

If the college or university does offer a credit card payment option, you will need to address this in your policy. Some, if not all, of your employees may wish to pay with personal credit cards in order to get the points associated with those payments. Whether or not you mandate the use of the corporate card is a policy question each organization will need to address on its own.

Tips for Medium or Smaller Organizations

Perhaps you don't have the travel spend that enables you to negotiate with travel providers for discounts. There still may be opportunities for you:

- Do a number of your employees frequently visit the same location? If so, try and negotiate a better rate with a local hotel in the area in exchange for requiring that all your travelers to that area use that location. Even if they will not lower the rates, they may throw in something such as free Internet access or breakfast for your employees.
- When sending an employee to a conference in a resort location or a big city, don't overlook special packages put together for vacationers. Often the package rate will be better than what you'll pay for the airfare and hotel separately, even if the employee doesn't use any of the special passes thrown in to entice vacationers. These deals may include transportation from the airport and/or breakfast, so there can be additional savings.

Don't overlook travel savings in your own backyard. If you have employees from other locations who frequently visit your office, negotiate a better rate with the local hotel. This can be offered to visitors to your location who come on company business. While it won't save your budget any money, it will endear you to your visitors.

15

BEST PRACTICES FOR THE ENTIRE T&E PROCESS

INTRODUCTION

While you might like to summarize your best practices by just telling your employees to use some common sense, if you've come this far in the book you know that will not always work. Organizations must walk a fine line. They need to incorporate practices that will provide their employees with the tools they need to complete business travel and entertainment (T&E) in an efficient manner without spending a fortune, hence the counsel not to spend a dollar to save a dime. This means you should not go overboard on your monitoring, looking for every possible nickel that an employee might have spent against the T&E policy.

The advent of Sarbanes-Oxley has raised the bar for all organizations when it comes to T&E preparation, review, and reimbursement. The policies must exhibit strong internal controls. What follows is a list of best practices that come from extensive research, as well as input from two industry professionals: InterplX's president and CEO, Chuck Buckner, and Expensewatch's CEO, Bill Vergantino.

Best Practice 1

Have a formal written T&E policy that:

- Is updated regularly, no less frequently than once a year
- Addresses all issues, leaving nothing to employee interpretation
- Is approved in writing by senior management
- Is distributed to all affected employees (possibly posted on the corporate intranet site)
- Is uniformly enforced

Best Practice 2

Have consequences for not doing what the policy requires. Specifically there need to be consequences for:

- Nonsubmittal (no card; taxable income, etc.) of expense reports
- Non-timely submission of expense reports
- Policy noncompliance
- Fraud

As with other parts of the policy, this practice should be uniformly enforced. This is an area that sometimes causes trouble. If one employee is let go and another valued employee is given the opportunity to make restitution or the matter is overlooked, that sends the wrong message and can put the organization in jeopardy of a lawsuit.

Best Practice 3

Do not verify every detail on every expense report. That is a lot of effort for not much dollar savings, given what you are likely to find. Exactly how much checking is adequate is open to discussion, with some experts recommending as little as 5% if there is a large universe of travelers and others recommending 20%. Those checked each month should include:

- Employees known to have abused the policy in the past
- All high-level executives
- All reports over a certain dollar level (to be set by each organization)
- A certain number of random reports

Best Practice 4

Each year the reports of several employees (some rogue spenders, some executives, and some randomly selected) should be pulled for the prior 14 months and each employee's reviewed as a package. Do any contain the same receipt? Do any contain sequentially numbered receipts? Can you identify any other patterns that might indicate fraud? Sometimes these trends are not easily identifiable when the reports are looked at by themselves but will jump out at you when viewed as a complete package.

Best Practice 5

Avoid certain practices that tend to be inefficient and weaken controls. These might include:

- Giving cash advances
- Allowing employees to pick up their expense reimbursement checks
- Not requiring that employees use the corporate T&E card

Best Practice 6

If your volume warrants it, make use of an automated expense preparation, review, and reimbursement system. This should incorporate policy compliance matching to prevent policy violations. It should automate the business rules as to who can review and approve transactions and should include e-mail notifications and transaction tracking mechanisms to reduce the approval cycle time.

Best Practice 7

If an automated system is used, integrate the corporate card data to prepopulate employees' expense report forms as well as capture the card data related to spend for negotiation and budget purposes.

Best Practice 8

Automate the collection and storage of receipts and other documentation, ideally having this scanned by the employee at the local level. This information should be attached (possibly through the use of a bar code) to the original report. All the document and receipt electronic processes should conform to the IRS regulations.

Best Practice 9

Those with a reasonable amount of international travel should incorporate processes that will enable the identification of VAT (value-added tax) reclaimable expenses. The programs should be structured and instructions given to employees traveling internationally so they can procure the proper documentation that will allow the VAT to be reclaimed.

Best Practice 10

Periodically, contracts with all preferred service providers should be reviewed and put out for bid to determine whether there is another provider of comparable service that will provide it at a lower cost. Competition can be stiff for lucrative corporate business travel contracts.

Best Practice 11

Don't forget about the rebates available if a corporate card is used. These can be rolled into one with the corporate purchasing card for the maximum rebate or separated on a T&E card split from the corporate card, if the organization is concerned about liability issues. In either event, ask for the rebate and make this one of the issues when you shop for a new card.

Best Practice 12

Require reimbursements to be made electronically to a bank account designated by the employee. It is possible to make this account separate from the account where the employee has his or her payroll deposited.

Best Practice 13

Keep your eye on the booking portals. There are tremendous changes taking place in the booking arena. This is the sleeper

T&E issue and could be the place where the next innovations come from. Don't get caught napping.

With the dollars involved for most organizations, the T&E process is one that deserves scrutiny and controls. Not only are there often large dollars involved, these expenses are unfortunately often spent in small increments, making it a nightmare to monitor. It is an arena that has experienced and will continue to experience monumental shifts in policies and procedures. What is considered a best practice one day quickly becomes an accepted mode of doing business.

Thus, it is imperative that even after you build the very best process you continue to monitor improvements and innovations in the marketplace. That, alas, is the fate of professionals charged with monitoring and making recommendations about the T&E practices in their organizations.

Appendix A

GSA PER DIEMS

STATE	CITY	BREAKFAST	LUNCH	DINNER	TOTAL
AK	All	$6	$ 9	$19	$34
AL	Birmingham	$7	$10	$21	$38
AL	Huntsville	$7	$10	$21	$38
AL	Mobile	$7	$10	$21	$38
AL	Other	$6	$ 9	$19	$34
AZ	Other	$6	$ 9	$19	$34
AZ	Phoenix	$7	$10	$21	$38
AZ	Scottsdale	$7	$10	$21	$38
CA	Anaheim	$9	$12	$25	$46
CA	Barstow	$7	$10	$21	$38
CA	Bridgeport	$7	$10	$21	$38
CA	Death Valley	$7	$10	$21	$38
CA	Fresno	$7	$10	$21	$38
CA	Gualala	$7	$10	$21	$38
CA	Los Angeles	$9	$12	$25	$46
CA	Modesto	$7	$10	$21	$38
CA	Monterey	$7	$10	$21	$38
CA	Napa	$7	$10	$21	$38

GSA PER DIEMS

STATE	CITY	BREAKFAST	LUNCH	DINNER	TOTAL
CA	Oakland	$7	$10	$21	$38
CA	Ontario	$7	$10	$21	$38
CA	Other	$6	$ 9	$19	$34
CA	Palm Springs	$7	$10	$21	$38
CA	Palo Alto	$7	$10	$21	$38
CA	Point Arena	$7	$10	$21	$38
CA	Redding	$7	$10	$21	$38
CA	Redwood City	$7	$10	$21	$38
CA	Sacramento	$7	$10	$21	$38
CA	San Diego	$9	$12	$25	$46
CA	San Francisco	$9	$12	$25	$46
CA	San Jose	$7	$10	$21	$38
CA	San Luis Obispo	$7	$10	$21	$38
CA	San Mateo	$7	$10	$21	$38
CA	Santa Barbara	$7	$10	$21	$38
CA	Santa Cruz	$7	$10	$21	$38
CA	Santa Rosa	$7	$10	$21	$38
CA	So. Lake Tahoe	$7	$10	$21	$38
CA	Tahoe City	$7	$10	$21	$38
CA	Yosemite Nat'l. Park	$7	$10	$21	$38
CO	Aspen	$7	$10	$21	$38
CO	Boulder	$7	$10	$21	$38
CO	Denver	$7	$10	$21	$38
CO	Durango	$7	$10	$21	$38
CO	Keystone	$7	$10	$21	$38
CO	Other	$6	$ 9	$19	$34
CO	Silverthorne	$7	$10	$21	$38
CO	Telluride	$7	$10	$21	$38
CO	Vail	$7	$10	$21	$38
CT	Bridgeport	$7	$10	$21	$38

GSA Per Diems

State	City	Breakfast	Lunch	Dinner	Total
CT	Danbury	$7	$10	$21	$38
CT	Other	$6	$ 9	$19	$34
CT	Salisbury	$7	$10	$21	$38
DC	Other	$6	$ 9	$19	$34
DC	Washington	$9	$12	$25	$46
DE	Other	$6	$ 9	$19	$34
DE	Wilmington	$7	$10	$21	$38
FL	Fort Myers	$7	$10	$21	$38
FL	Key West	$7	$10	$21	$38
FL	Miami	$7	$10	$21	$38
FL	Miami Beach	$7	$10	$21	$38
FL	Naples	$7	$10	$21	$38
FL	Other	$6	$ 9	$19	$34
FL	St. Petersburg	$7	$10	$21	$38
FL	Tampa	$7	$10	$21	$38
FL	West Palm Beach	$7	$10	$21	$38
GA	Atlanta	$7	$10	$21	$38
GA	Other	$6	$ 9	$19	$34
HI	All	$7	$10	$21	$38
ID	Ketchum	$7	$10	$21	$38
ID	Other	$6	$ 9	$19	$34
ID	Sun Valley	$7	$10	$21	$38
IL	Chicago	$9	$12	$25	$46
IL	Other	$6	$ 9	$19	$34
IL	Rockford	$7	$10	$21	$38
IN	Carmel	$7	$10	$21	$38
IN	Indianapolis	$7	$10	$21	$38
IN	Other	$6	$ 9	$19	$34
KS	Kansas City	$7	$10	$21	$38
KS	Other	$6	$ 9	$19	$34

GSA Per Diems

STATE	CITY	BREAKFAST	LUNCH	DINNER	TOTAL
KY	Covington	$7	$10	$21	$38
KY	Louisville	$7	$10	$21	$38
KY	Other	$6	$ 9	$19	$34
LA	New Orleans	$7	$10	$21	$38
LA	Other	$6	$ 9	$19	$34
MA	Andover	$7	$10	$21	$38
MA	Boston	$9	$12	$25	$46
MA	Cambridge	$7	$10	$21	$38
MA	Hyannis	$7	$10	$21	$38
MA	Lowell	$7	$10	$21	$38
MA	Martha's Vineyard	$7	$10	$21	$38
MA	Nantucket	$7	$10	$21	$38
MA	Other	$6	$ 9	$19	$34
MA	Quincy	$7	$10	$21	$38
MD	Annapolis	$7	$10	$21	$38
MD	Baltimore	$7	$10	$21	$38
MD	Columbia	$7	$10	$21	$38
MD	Fredrick	$7	$10	$21	$38
MD	Ocean City	$7	$10	$21	$38
MD	Other	$6	$ 9	$19	$34
ME	Other	$6	$ 9	$19	$34
ME	Portland	$7	$10	$21	$38
MI	Detroit	$9	$12	$25	$46
MI	Mackinac Island	$7	$10	$21	$38
MI	Other	$6	$ 9	$19	$34
MI	Pontiac	$7	$10	$21	$38
MI	Port Huron	$7	$10	$21	$38
MI	Troy	$7	$10	$21	$38
MN	Duluth	$7	$10	$21	$38
MN	Minneapolis	$7	$10	$21	$38

GSA Per Diems

State	City	Breakfast	Lunch	Dinner	Total
MN	Other	$6	$ 9	$19	$34
MN	St. Paul	$7	$10	$21	$38
MO	Kansas City	$7	$10	$21	$38
MO	Other	$6	$ 9	$19	$34
MO	St. Louis	$7	$10	$21	$38
MS	Other	$6	$ 9	$19	$34
MS	Ridgeland	$7	$10	$21	$38
NC	Chapel Hill	$7	$10	$21	$38
NC	Charlotte	$7	$10	$21	$38
NC	Durham	$7	$10	$21	$38
NC	Other	$6	$ 9	$19	$34
NC	Raleigh	$7	$10	$21	$38
NH	Hanover	$7	$10	$21	$38
NH	Lebanon	$7	$10	$21	$38
NH	Other	$6	$ 9	$19	$34
NJ	Atlantic City	$7	$10	$21	$38
NJ	Camden	$7	$10	$21	$38
NJ	Dover	$7	$10	$21	$38
NJ	Edison	$7	$10	$21	$38
NJ	Moorestown	$7	$10	$21	$38
NJ	Newark	$7	$10	$21	$38
NJ	Other	$6	$ 9	$19	$34
NJ	Parsippany	$7	$10	$21	$38
NJ	Princeton	$7	$10	$21	$38
NJ	Trenton	$7	$10	$21	$38
NM	Albuquerque	$7	$10	$21	$38
NM	Other	$6	$ 9	$19	$34
NM	Santa Fe	$7	$10	$21	$38
NV	Incline Village	$7	$10	$21	$38
NV	Las Vegas	$7	$10	$21	$38

GSA Per Diems

State	City	Breakfast	Lunch	Dinner	Total
NV	Other	$6	$ 9	$19	$34
NV	Stateline	$7	$10	$?1	$38
NY	Albany	$7	$10	$21	$38
NY	Buffalo	$7	$10	$21	$38
NY	Glens Falls	$7	$10	$21	$38
NY	New York City	$9	$12	$25	$46
NY	Other	$6	$ 9	$19	$34
NY	Rochester	$7	$10	$21	$38
NY	Saratoga Springs	$7	$10	$21	$38
NY	Schenectady	$7	$10	$21	$38
NY	White Plains	$7	$10	$21	$38
OH	Akron	$7	$10	$21	$38
OH	Cleveland	$7	$10	$21	$38
OH	Columbus	$7	$10	$21	$38
OH	Other	$6	$ 9	$19	$34
OR	Ashland	$7	$10	$21	$38
OR	Lincoln City	$7	$10	$21	$38
OR	Medford	$7	$10	$21	$38
OR	Newport	$7	$10	$21	$38
OR	Other	$6	$ 9	$19	$34
OR	Portland	$7	$10	$21	$38
PA	Allentown	$7	$10	$21	$38
PA	Chester	$7	$10	$21	$38
PA	Fort Washington	$7	$10	$21	$38
PA	Harrisburg	$7	$10	$21	$38
PA	King of Prussia	$7	$10	$21	$38
PA	Other	$6	$ 9	$19	$34
PA	Philadelphia	$7	$10	$21	$38
PA	Pittsburgh	$7	$10	$21	$38
PA	Radnor	$7	$10	$21	$38
RI	Newport	$7	$10	$21	$38

GSA Per Diems

STATE	CITY	BREAKFAST	LUNCH	DINNER	TOTAL
RI	Providence	$7	$10	$21	$38
SC	Greenville	$7	$10	$21	$38
SC	Holton Head	$7	$10	$21	$38
TN	Nashville	$7	$10	$21	$38
TX	Austin	$7	$10	$21	$38
TX	Dallas	$7	$10	$21	$38
TX	Fort Worth	$7	$10	$21	$38
TX	Galveston	$7	$10	$21	$38
TX	Houston	$7	$10	$21	$38
UT	Park City	$7	$10	$21	$38
UT	Salt Lake City	$7	$10	$21	$38
VA	Alexandria	$7	$10	$21	$38
VA	Arlington	$9	$12	$25	$46
VA	Charlottesville	$7	$10	$21	$38
VA	Chesapeake	$7	$10	$21	$38
VA	Fairfax	$7	$10	$21	$38
VA	Falls Church	$7	$10	$21	$38
VA	Hampton	$7	$10	$21	$38
VA	Newport News	$7	$10	$21	$38
VA	Norfolk	$7	$10	$21	$38
VA	Portsmouth	$7	$10	$21	$38
VA	Richmond	$7	$10	$21	$38
VA	Virginia Beach	$7	$10	$21	$38
VA	Williamsburg	$7	$10	$21	$38
VA	Wintergreen	$7	$10	$21	$38
WA	Seattle	$7	$10	$21	$38
WA	Spokane	$7	$10	$21	$38
WA	Vancouver	$7	$10	$21	$38
WI	Brookfield	$7	$10	$21	$38
WI	Wisconsin Dells	$7	$10	$21	$38
WY	Jackson	$7	$10	$21	$38

Appendix B

VAT Rates for Selected Countries				
Country	Hotel	Meals	Car Rental	Conferences Training Seminars Trade Shows	
Austria	10	10	N/A	20	20
Belgium	6	21	21	21	21
Canada	7/6.5	N/A	N/A	7	N/A
Denmark	25	25	N/A	25	25
Finland	8	N/A	22	22	22
France	5.5	19.6/5.5	N/A	19.6	19.6
Germany	16	16/7	16	16	16
Ireland	N/A	N/A	N/A	21	21
Italy	N/A	N/A	20	20/10	20
Korea	10	10	10	10	10
Netherlands	6	N/A	19	19	19
Norway	0	N/A	N/A	25	0
Spain	16/7	16/7	16	7	16
Sweden	12	25	25	25	25
Switzerland	3.6	7.6	7.6	7.6	7.6
UK	17.5	17.5	17.5	17.5	17.5

N/A = VAT not recoverable in these countries for this item.

INDEX